THEATRE SYMPOSIUM
A PUBLICATION OF THE SOUTHEASTERN THEATRE CONFERENCE

Theatre and the Popular

Volume 31

Published by the

Southeastern Theatre Conference and

The University of Alabama Press

EDITORS

EDITOR

Chase Bringardner
Auburn University

ASSOCIATE EDITOR

Sunny Stalter-Pace
Auburn University

EDITORIAL BOARD

Becky K. Becker
Clemson University

Gregory S. Carr
Harris-Stowe State University

J. K. Curry
Wake Forest University

Philip G. Hill
Furman University

Andy Gibb
Texas Tech University

Eve Graves
Clark Atlanta University

Keith Byron Kirk
Virginia Commonwealth University

Sarah McCarroll
Georgia Southern University

Scott Phillips
Auburn University

David S. Thompson
Agnes Scott College

E. Bert Wallace
Campbell University

Copyright © 2024 The University of Alabama Press

Cover illustration: View of the dance floor during the preshow for Project 400 Theater's *The Donkey Show*, American Repertory Theater, Cambridge; photo by Marcus Stern.

THEATRE SYMPOSIUM (ISSN 1065-4917) is published annually by The University of Alabama Press, Box 870380, Tuscaloosa, AL 35487–0380. Subscription rates for 2024 are $25.00 for individuals and $35.00 for institutions; please include an additional $10.00 for subscriptions outside the United States. Back issues are $34.95.

Paperback ISBN: 978–0-8173–7018-3
eBook ISBN: 978–0-8173–9521-6

THEATRE SYMPOSIUM is published annually by the Southeastern Theatre Conference, Inc. (SETC), and by the University of Alabama Press. SETC nonstudent members receive the journal as a part of their membership under rules determined by SETC. For information on membership, visit the SETC website at www.setc.org, send an email to info@setc.org, or write to Southeastern Theatre Conference, 5710 W. Gate City Boulevard, Suite K, Box 186, Greensboro, NC 27407. All other inquiries regarding subscriptions, circulation, purchase of individual copies, and requests to reprint materials should be addressed to Accounting Specialist, University of Alabama Press, Box 870380, Tuscaloosa, AL 35487–0380.

THEATRE SYMPOSIUM publishes works of scholarship resulting from a single-topic meeting held on a southeastern university campus each spring. A call for papers to be presented at that meeting is widely publicized each autumn for the following spring. Information about the next symposium is available from Keith Byron Kirk, Virginia Commonwealth University, Department of Theatre, School of the Arts, 325 North Harrison Street, Box 842519, Richmond, VA 23284–519, kbkirk@vcu.edu.

THEATRE SYMPOSIUM
A PUBLICATION OF THE SOUTHEASTERN THEATRE CONFERENCE

Volume 31   *Contents*   **2024**

Ethos Statement	vii
Introduction Chase Bringardner	1
Popular Performance and Everyday Life: Interdisciplinary Transnational Dispatches from the Street and Sea Janet M. Davis	6
Unpopular Populism: Project 400 Theater's LES Travesti Tom Fish	18
Ndangered Narratives: Ernie McClintock as an Early Facilitator of Hip-Hop Theatre Elizabeth M. Cizmar	33
Performing Pilgrimage: Popular Religious Education at Chautauqua's Palestine Park Chelsea Taylor	46
Subculture or Pop Culture? Theatre, Fashion, and Air Guitar Kyla Kazuschyk	61
Staging Black Popularity: *One Night in Miami* and the Historic Hampton House Mysia Anderson	72
The Popularity of Contemporary Singaporean Pantomime Chelsea Curto	87
Promoting a Popular Body: The Stage, Couture, and the Creation of the Female Form in the Late Nineteenth and Early Twentieth Centuries Sarah McCarroll	100
Trauma from a Safe Distance: The Unprecedented Success of *The History of the Troubles (Accordin' to My Da)* Eleanor Owicki	113
Pugilists, Ponies, and Propriety: A Micro-History of Popular Athleticism at the Local Opera House Chris Woodworth	126
Contributors	143

Ethos Statement

Theatre Symposium is resolutely committed to equity, diversity, inclusion, and accessibility in creating a space for theatre scholarship, and we are actively engaged in equity, diversity, inclusion, and justice (EDIJ) work as a valued practice within our activities as scholars and practitioners of theatre. We embrace work representing a diverse spectrum of writing styles, editorial perspectives, performance types, and critical analyses. In choosing personnel, managing the peer review process, and planning our annual event and subsequent journal, *Theatre Symposium* seeks opportunities to center the voices, bodies, and stories of the global majority.

Introduction

Chase Bringardner

THE THIRTY-FIRST VOLUME of *Theatre Symposium, Theatre & The Popular*, documents conversations that traverse disciplinary boundaries, moving between theatre, performance, and American studies to interrogate exciting networks of ideas around the idea of the popular. Over the course of our three-day, April 2022 gathering at Agnes Scott College, attendees interrogated what constitutes the popular, what popular looks like, and what popular entails regarding performance. We explored how the popular is performed and how theatre engages with (or even creates) the popular over time. We considered historical frameworks and the ongoing role of performance in framing ideas and conversations about the popular and popularity. We investigated the relationship between the popular and performance in an increasingly frenetic and mediated landscape. We gathered together to interrogate these ideas against the backdrop of the urgency of this current moment of recycled, reemergent populist discourse and the continued oversized presence of popular culture in our everyday lives.

Considerations of the popular occur onstage and off, backstage and front of house, and throughout various configurations of audience. What is considered popular, how that determination gets made, and who makes it shapes the very structures and systems of theatre and performance in professional contexts as well as in communities and academic environments. Theatre engages the popular, and the popular engages theatre. Many productions succeed or fail based on their ability to align with what is popular, sometimes productively, sometimes clumsily, sometimes brazenly, and sometimes tragically.

In the current moment, what constitutes the popular has profound real-world impacts, politically, economically, and socially. Debates around the feasibility of the electoral college system hinge on a perception of the power and potential of the "popular" vote. Streaming services daily update lists of their most popular content and base future decisions on opaque measures of popularity. Social media provides avenues for the creation of content that rapidly circulates across the globe, generating views and clicks for new products, political revolutions, and social activism all on the same screen. We grapple with the still-lingering impact of the COVID-19 global pandemic that destabilized the means of production and shifted the ways humans create community and engage with culture writ large. Combined with emerging technologies, these changes continue to alter points of access and open up new pathways to the popular. Remember *Tiger King*? The popular is often fleeting by its very nature and requires systems and mechanisms to sustain that popularity. Organizations like the Southeastern Theatre Conference (SETC) itself continue to wrestle with the implications of these changes as they attempt to "remain popular" and responsive through shifts and pivots to meet the needs of its members while also reconsidering the very nature of membership itself.

The editors and contributors to this volume respond to these and the multitudes of questions that arise in this moment. They engage with a range of examples, contemporary and historical, and argue with urgent clarity and intellectual acuity and nuance for exploring the interplay of performance and the popular. As the work in this volume demonstrates, theatre and performance deeply engage with the popular at almost every level, from audience response to box office revenue. The variety of methodologies and sites of inquiry showcased in this volume demonstrates the breadth and depth of the popular and the importance of such work to understanding our present moment onstage and off.

After a year of convening virtually due to the ongoing COVID pandemic, this volume emerges from our return to an in-person meeting. We returned to the campus of Agnes Scott College in Decatur, Georgia, gathering together to hear our keynote speaker, Janet M. Davis, deliver her address and to listen to participants present papers in progress and exchange ideas and feedback over food and beverage. The return to our usual format allowed people to share their work and receive feedback in formal and informal settings. Conversations spilled over from the classroom to the lobby and then to the restaurants (and bars) of downtown Decatur. Over the course of that weekend in April, nearly thirty people listened to Janet M. Davis's provocative keynote speech and presented their work in a series of curated, themed panels with ample time devoted for discussion and the building of community. The contributions to this volume emerged from this invigorating weekend, and the scope and range of topics covered by these articles demonstrates the exciting possibilities, in both content and form, inherent in such inquiries into the popular.

Janet M. Davis's opening essay sets the tone for the entire volume. As the keynote for this gathering, Davis skillfully lays out the terms of engagement, considering the term "popular" across disciplinary boundaries and within a variety of theoretical frameworks. She playfully weaves her own personal and professional narratives together with a consideration of theatre and the popular, resulting in a meditation on how the frameworks of the popular and performance traverse multiple geographies. Davis cleverly divides her piece into "the street" and "the sea," illustrating how her own treatment of the circus and the film *Jaws* and its reception, respectively, demonstrates the powerful potential of popular analysis to lay bare the ways culture shapes our reality.

Tom Fish and Elizabeth M. Cizmar pick up threads of Davis's analysis, offering essays that expand notions of the popular, specifically focusing, though in different ways, on New York City. Fish introduces the concept of "unpopular populism" as it relates to Project 400 Theater's ambitious though ultimately unsuccessful attempt to produce four hundred projects conceived in the "scrappy, resourceful model of LES [Lower East Side] theatrical populism." Through vivid documentation of *The Donkey Show*, their adaptation of *A Midsummer Night's Dream*, Fish's analysis delves into the contested nature of a popular where "progressive grassroots strategies" come into conflict with commercial pressures. A similar tension emerges in Cizmar's essay, which argues for the important contributions of Ernie McClintock to both the Black Arts Movement and hip-hop theatre. McClintock's positionality and his communal and collective performance strategies, while subverting hegemony, leave him out of many popular narratives of the history of hip-hop theatre. Both Cizmar's and Fish's work highlights the tensions between the popular and the progressive, in terms of efficacy as well as documentation and memory.

The next essays in the volume, while they grapple with very different examples, pick up on these themes of documentation and memory and argue for the inclusion of live performance as a generator of popularity. Chelsea Taylor's piece looks at the Chautauqua Assembly's replica of the Holy Land titled Park of Palestine and argues that the site's popularity "during the late-nineteenth and early-twentieth centuries was inherently tied to performances within the park." The presence of live performance afforded audiences the opportunity for embodied engagement with the site, walking (figuratively) where Jesus walked. Similarly, Kyla Kazuschyk's essay emphasizes the importance of embodied performance in explaining the popularity of air guitar as documented and staged in the play *Airness*. In both examples, the authors make compelling arguments for the theatricality of these quite disparate sites of performance and identify the presence of live performers functioning as audience surrogates as integral to their popularity.

Building on conversations around the popular and sites of performance, Mysia Anderson and Chelsea Curto in their essays configure popular performance itself as a way to rethink or reconfigure space. Anderson's piece chronicles the significance of The Hampton House, a Green Book hotel in Miami,

Florida, and its representation in both the play and the film *One Night in Miami*. Anderson argues that the popular film and stage play belie the fullness of the embodied space of the actual Hampton House and its rich history. Moreover, Anderson argues that the popularity of the participants in that famous evening in the hotel—Malcolm X, Cassius Clay, Sam Cooke, and Jim Brown—leads to an erasure of the significance of the physical space itself and calls for a return to a more embodied sense of this significant historical space. Curto's essay likewise thinks through the way popular performance negotiates space, in this case highlighting how Singaporean pantomime creates space onstage for considerations of identity in relation to legacies of British colonialism. For Curto, Singaporean pantomime "requires an audience to articulate who they are as a nation" and uses popular performance as a means to make real the spaces of identity formation in postcolonial Singapore.

Within the final three essays, Sarah McCarroll, Eleanor Owicki, and Chris Woodworth expand on the previous discussion of space to interrogate in different ways how the popular gets established, maintained, and regulated. McCarroll provides the rich example of popular fashion in the late Victorian and Edwardian periods and stage performers' role in creating and circulating the "popular body." She emphasizes the useful tension inherent in the arrangement wherein "the bodies and the clothing [performers] wear must at one and the same time feed the demand for what is already popular . . . while also retaining the power to present the embodied shapes and styles that will (re)create the new, next popular bodies and fashions." These performers' bodies, according to McCarroll, exist in an almost liminal, transitory space, embodying the popular while simultaneously anticipating and creating its next iteration.

Unlike the circulation of a popular body in the late Victorian and Edwardian period onstage and in print, the popularity of *The History of the Troubles (Accordin' to My Da)* across the early 2000s in Ireland emerges from a different context. In her essay, Owicki explores the reasons for the unprecedented success of this play, which purports to document an incredibly harrowing and grim period of Irish history using familiarity and humor. While McCarroll details the proliferation and circulation of actor's bodies onstage and in print to account for the popular, Owicki emphasizes the importance of the circulation of an embodied, lived experience in this play "to construct a comfortable familiarity rooted in shared experience." The popularity of *The History of the Troubles (Accordin' to My Da)* results from a desire for a collective experience while also illustrating the importance of shared context to the establishment and maintenance of the popular.

Similar to Owicki, Chris Woodworth's essay starts with a comparable premise—to determine why performances featuring boxers and equestrians achieved high levels of popularity at the Smith's Opera House in Geneva, New York, in the late nineteenth and early twentieth centuries. Woodworth's essay provides an appropriate concluding piece for this volume as it pulls together many previous threads running through the other contributions, tracing the origins of popularity through a multifaceted approach that proves the rule that more than one thing can be true at the same time. In the case of live popular performance, a complex network of sometimes seemingly contradictory forces interacts at the site of performance to make meaning. The popularity of these performances was rooted in appeals both to exciting physical feats and to the reassuring presence of moralizing and uplift.

The yearly gathering and the publication of *Theatre Symposium* would certainly not be possible without the continued support of the Southeastern Theatre Conference. Maegan Azar, SETC's now immediate past president, provided sound guidance and steady leadership throughout these past years as the organization and symposium itself transitioned from the virtual to the in-person. Her vision for SETC inspires us and encourages us to continue to strive for the best, most accessible, and most expansive understanding of theatre and performance scholarship. I want to thank her personally for her labor and her support of our many efforts.

I am also grateful to the entire *Theatre Symposium* steering committee and editorial board for the wisdom and guidance they provided in this, my second year as editor. They helped me to guide this symposium and volume as we returned to Agnes Scott and entered a new phase of the COVID pandemic. I am particularly grateful to Andy Gibb, who I served under for two years as associate editor, and to Sarah McCarroll and Becky Becker, who welcomed me so graciously to *Theatre Symposium* during their editorships. Their grace, dedication, passion, humor, and kindness continue to inspire me in my own work.

Offering generous counsel and a wealth of editorial experience, my associate editor, Sunny Salter-Pace, served as a wonderfully gracious and engaged collaborator. Her intellect, curiosity, and compassion greatly enhanced everyone's efforts, and her generous and astute feedback allowed each author to grow and shape their ideas in exciting ways. I am thankful for her many efforts and friendship.

Finally, I must thank my home institution, the Department of Theatre and Dance at Auburn University. They have encouraged me in so many ways throughout my editorship. The kindness, guidance, and care of my colleagues and friends, both within the department and across campus, allowed me to take on this project with clear eyes and a full heart.

Keynote Lecture

Popular Performance and Everyday Life

Interdisciplinary Transnational Dispatches from the Street and Sea

Janet M. Davis

MY SCHOLARSHIP AS a cultural, social, and environmental historian explores the complex relationships between theatre and the popular among human and nonhuman animals over time. My interdisciplinary theoretical and methodological tool kit treats "theatre" as an expansive, historically situated cultural form whose structures of ephemeral performance and performativity spill outside the physical boundaries of the stage into the street, market, home, school, beach, sea, countryside, and other informal arenas of daily life—in settings that range from the intimate to the transnational. Similarly, I consider the "popular" to be an artifact of lived experience: accessible, sensory, affective, and made material either by hand or via mass-production by machines. Further, the popular is a central site of intersectional social conflict, or in the words of cultural studies theorist Stuart Hall, "contested terrain," where struggles related to national belonging and exclusion are fought.[1]

Raymond Williams, a longtime professor of drama at Cambridge, conceived of cultural history as a social material process that symbiotically connects the material base and ideological superstructure. He turned to etymology to make sense of the dynamic material history of "culture," in what he describes as "the growth and tending of crops and animals, and by extension the growth and tending of human faculties," which illuminates inextricable connections among the human and nonhuman worlds in thinking about culture and the popular, more specifically.[2] Historian Robin D. G. Kelley embraces political anthropologist James C. Scott's term "infrapolitics" to analyze the cumulative relationship between daily acts of popular resistance among dispossessed people and social change. Making popular culture material and performative, Kelley explores public transportation during World War II in Birmingham, Alabama, as "moving theaters." According to Kelley, "theater can have two meanings: as a site of performance and as a site of military conflict."[3] Kelley observes how buses became theatres of conflict as Black working-class residents repeatedly refused to give up their seats to white passengers—often at the risk of serious injury or death.

Embracing Kelley's dual homonymic meanings of "theatre" in this essay, I will examine three cultural and social formations—the circus, animal protectionism, and a famous shark movie—to analyze the synergetic relationships between theatre and the popular on the street and sea. Before I move into these specific areas of discussion, I hope that you, dear reader, will permit a bit of autobiographical reflection on a few key moments that have shaped my approach to interdisciplinary scholarship.

One of my early encounters with theatre and the popular occurred while watching television. In the summer of 1972, I interrupted my usual fare of *The Brady Bunch*, *The Partridge Family*, *All in the Family*, and *The Carol Burnett Show*, to watch *The Six Wives of Henry VIII*, which aired each week on *Masterpiece Theatre*. Glued to our Sony Trinitron, I was riveted by King Henry's obsessive desire for a male heir, the precarious status of his six wives, the religious upheaval of the Reformation, and the rich sensorium that saturated each episode with recorders, lutes, harpsichords, and opulent costumes of brocade, silk, and velvet, fitted bodices, gable headdresses, French hoods, and jewelry. Unhappily, my history classes in primary and secondary school were boring enumerations of dates and political facts that bore little resemblance to the complex, roiling affective universe of *The Six Wives of Henry VIII*. While I read everything I could about Tudor history, my interest in the performative, popular, and everyday cultural worlds from the distant past remained unaddressed until college. There, my history professors dove directly into the intersectional meanings of bread and culture; music of the dead and epidemiology during the Black Death; Bakhtin and Carnival; American Cold War monster movies; and South Asian art and architecture as an expression of Hindu, Mughal, and British power in India.

In 1984, I lived in Pune, India, during my junior year of college. The sensory worlds of theatre and the popular permeated my daily life, in part, because my host family's flat was right next to Vijay Talkies, a Marathi-language movie theatre, where the syncopations of tabla drums, sitar, and strings from cinematic soundtracks punctuated our conversations. Considerations of theatre and the popular structured my formal education in India, as well. I conducted a research project on a social movement led by a local Hindu businessman to teach women how to perform Vedic purification rites and special prayers from the Rig Veda—a practice previously forbidden by the male priesthood. I interviewed *riskikas* (priestesses) and Shankar Hari Thatte, the elderly Chitpawan Brahman businessman who led this movement to combat a male priesthood that he charged was "cheating people."[4] As I dug into my research, I learned that many participants were part of the Bharatiya Janata Party (BJP), a new political party dedicated to a Hindu nationalist future for India. (The BJP's current leader, Narendra Modi, has been India's prime minister since 2014.) This project redoubled my excitement for scholarly research. A year later, my senior honors thesis explored the relationship between Indo-Saracenic architecture and imperialism in India; my research introduced me to Edward Said's best-known work, *Orientalism*, and the vibrant fields of postcolonial studies and cultural studies, which, to this day, illuminate the contested ideological meanings of cultural processes, productions, and performances.[5] I was excited for a scholarly future. But I wasn't ready just yet.

Consequently, I spent the next three years in a crisp eggplant wool/poly uniform as a flight attendant for Northwest Airlines, where my labor aboard the airplane constituted another realm of performance—with strict dress, hair, and makeup regulations that had to be approved by a supervisor at my base in Detroit before each trip. But when flying with friends away from the watchful eyes of management, I found plenty of space for fun, jokes on carefully chosen passengers possessing a sense of humor, and camaraderie in the sky. I also learned how to be ready to travel at a moment's notice and to conceal my emotions behind a friendly smile, a signature of what the sociologist Arlie Hochschild calls "emotional labor" in the workplace.[6] (This skill became particularly useful when I later was appointed department chair.) The experience of relentless travel also—unknowingly at the time—prepared me for my dissertation on traveling circuses.

I entered graduate school in modern South Asian history in 1989. I had planned to build upon my undergraduate research on theatre and the popular through the study of parades and ceremonial durbars as a portal into imperial popular culture and political ideologies during the British Raj. But my plans changed one day at the Museum of Science and Industry in Chicago when I discovered a pictorial exhibit of American circus parades from the turn of the twentieth century. The photographs chronicled thousands of people lining the streets and peering out of second- and third-story windows to watch processions of horses, camels, gilded wagons containing wild animals, and elephants caparisoned with howdahs driven by mahouts in brownface in towns and cities across the country.

The parade scenes of these photographs bore a striking resemblance to the Orientalist colonial popular culture I was studying in graduate school. I kept thinking about the American circus all summer long as I completed a Hindi language program in Varanasi, India. In the spring of 1991, I transferred into the American history PhD program at the University of Wisconsin-Madison, conveniently located just forty miles away from Baraboo, home to the world's largest public circus archive at Circus World Museum.

My research showed that the growth and expansion of American circus was actively wedded to the nation's ideological and material transformation into a modern industrial society with a burgeoning overseas empire. During the Gilded Age and Progressive Era, circus owners, such as P. T. Barnum, became celebrity capitalists who engaged in mergers and acquisitions of rival shows. They saw themselves as impresarios of respectability because they offered audiences educational, if titillating, entertainment drawn from a world beyond provincial borders. Traveling via railroad by the 1870s, the nation's largest tented circuses became huge "traveling towns" that employed more than one thousand people from around the world, featured hundreds of animals, and could accommodate more than ten thousand spectators under a voluminous canvas big top that contained three rings, two stages, and an outer hippodrome track—all of which were simultaneous sites of meticulously coordinated performances.[7]

The Street

On "Circus Day," performances of human and animal labor extended far beyond the ring. Laborers performed disciplined spectacles of erecting and disassembling the canvas city, a display of synchronous bodily labor that attracted spectators to the "greatest free show on earth." This spectacle of labor began at the rail yard before dawn on Circus Day, where crowds flocked to witness the workers, or roustabouts, unload the train cars. A few hours later, thousands of people poured into the streets to watch the parade.[8]

The street was, perhaps, the most socially unpredictable site of performance on Circus Day. Towns often swelled with ten to fifteen thousand additional "strangers" as area residents from neighboring hamlets plodded on foot, by horse, or by special railroad "excursion fares" that were discounted in honor of the ritual occasion.[9] Schools and factories shuttered so that restive children and weary workers could attend the show. But local shops remained open to offer Circus Day bargain prices to the thousands of potential customers flocking to Main Street for the free street parade. On September 29, 1899, for example, the *Barton County Democrat* in Great Bend, Kansas, advertised its upcoming Circus Day prices on men's suits, ladies' gloves, underwear, boys' clothing, kerchiefs, shoes, suspenders, blankets, lemon drops, cheese, coffee, Bromo-Seltzer, bulk starch, olive soap, wood butter molds, Carter's Little Liver Pills, food choppers, syrup of figs, and Hall's Catarrh Cure—among many other goods.[10]

Emily Dickinson observed the ways in which the circus's jarring breakdown of human and animal boundaries in its performances was replicated in the streets during the parade: "The show is not the show, / But they that go. / Menagerie to me / My neighbor be. / Fair play— / Both went to see."[11] Dickinson bore witness to the ways in which the heaving, sweaty crowds were transmogrified into a "menagerie to me," a spectacular, discombobulating, and unpredictable "show" that defamiliarized neighbors into strangers. The collective anonymity of many thousands in the streets on Circus Day tempted some people to steal, drink, or fight while the community was otherwise distracted by gilded wagons, brass bands, and charismatic megafauna.

The streets and showgrounds offered circusgoers opportunities for ritual celebration and community formation. Historian Sakina Hughes writes that the showgrounds were social spaces for African American families to gather, picnic, visit, gossip, and reconnect. Further, Hughes pays special attention to employment opportunities for Black musicians, such as sideshow bandleaders Walter Loving and Perry George "P. G." Lowery.[12] Although Jim Crow segregation structured social and cultural encounters in the turn-of-the-century South, the expansive and ephemeral showgrounds offered occasional points of racially integrated exchange and contact—even in those locations where local segregation laws dictated separate circus ticket windows, entrances, and standing areas in the pit (also known as the gallery).[13]

Nonetheless, performative spaces outside the ring and stage were often dangerous. Within minutes, crowds could become mobs. Lubricated by alcohol, the cloak of anonymity amid thousands of people, or the desire to settle scores with one's enemies, Circus Day on the street could be hazardous. Tenting circus route books (a show's diary of each show stop published at the conclusion of the season) and newspapers reveal the shocking constancy of racist mob violence on Circus Day. With deplorable frequency, local mob violence targeted African American circus workers.

On June 15, 1920, Duluth, Minnesota, was the scene of an atrocity. Immediately after the John Robinson Circus had performed its nighttime show on June 14, a local white man falsely accused six African American roustabouts (laborers) of raping a white woman at gunpoint behind the big top. The police immediately arrested the six men without probable cause and threw them in the downtown jail. At the same time, the circus rumbled off to its next date at Virginia, Minnesota, thus abandoning the six circus workers—leaving them at the mercy of local authorities. Duluth police were so frenzied by the accusations that they traveled to Virginia, where they arrested four more African American roustabouts on the show.

The news of the arrests traveled fast. By nightfall on June 15, an explosive white mob of approximately ten thousand people broke down doors and shattered windows as they stormed the city jail and seized Elias Clayton, Elmer

Jackson, and Isaac McGhie. The mob pushed the three circus workers outside into the roiling mob. The men endured a fake trial before they were murdered and lynched from a light pole at the corner of First Street and Second Avenue East. The *New York Times* reported a horrific scene of "revelry . . . like a crowd attending a carnival," noting that the mob disappeared at the same lightning speed with which it had formed.[14] The other roustabouts remained in jail and remained steadfast in their innocence. Soon thereafter, Max Mason was falsely convicted of rape and served four years in prison before he was pardoned on condition that he leave Minnesota. Three white men were convicted of causing a riot, and Minnesota passed an anti-lynching law in 1921. Yet, no perpetrator was brought to justice for the lynching of the three circus workers.[15] As a traveling form of theatre and the popular, the circus was a paradoxical touchstone of community consolidation and fragmentation in Jim Crow America.

As accessible and volatile public spaces, streets also have been a stage for popular movements. When a group of wealthy animal advocates in New York successfully incorporated their new organization, the American Society for the Prevention of Cruelty to Animals (ASPCA), at the New York Legislature in 1866, their leader, Henry Bergh, was highly attentive to the performative optics of staging and costuming. A playwright by aspiration more than profession, Bergh was the son of a shipbuilder who grew rich on government contracts during the War of 1812.[16] Although Bergh had been occupationally aimless for much of his adult life, President Lincoln chose him to serve as secretary of legation in St. Petersburg, Russia, from 1862 to 1864, owing to the elite standing of Bergh's family. Yet Bergh served for only two years because his health problems flared in the Russian cold. Still, his service in St. Petersburg marked a personal and professional watershed because he found his life's purpose after many decades of wandering. Like many other Americans, Bergh was conditioned to view Russia through the lens of American stereotypes of unmitigated brutality.[17] He often saw laboring animals being flogged, but Russian drivers ignored him when he told them to stop. People on the streets, by turns, jeered and bullied him. The turning point came when Bergh challenged an especially aggressive driver while outfitted in his court dress and fluttery legation ribbons. In contrast to earlier displays of utter disrespect, the driver, police, and crowds were courteous and fully cooperative, owing to Bergh's strategic performative use of his uniform, "At last I've found a way to utilize my gold lace and about the best use I can make of it."[18]

After he returned to the United States, Bergh rallied supporters with passionate speeches characterizing animal welfare as a universal moral cause. On April 10, 1866, the New York Legislature voted to incorporate the ASPCA. This law of incorporation granted the new organization extraordinary policing powers: Even though the SPCA was a private organization, its officers could legally arrest anyone on the streets caught flogging or neglecting an animal under the state's extant (but rarely enforced) anti-cruelty statute, passed in 1829.[19] Consequently, ASPCA officers wore police-like badges and uniforms.[20] Bergh's performative moment in St. Petersburg had stuck. On crowded city streets, the uniform was an instantly recognizable symbol of authority for the fledgling ASPCA. Until his death in 1888, Bergh stalked the city streets wearing his police-like overcoat and badge, as well as a top hat, which made him look even taller than his height of more than six feet. He was ubiquitous. In 1879, *Scribner's Monthly* noted, "Since Horace Greeley's death, no figure more familiar to the public has walked the streets of the metropolis."[21] Despite Bergh's desire to protect turtles, pigeons, and rabbits, he was primarily attuned to the welfare of the city's domestic laboring animals. Bergh reenacted dramatic scenes of surveillance and confrontation over a twenty-two-year period: He flashed his badge, physically placed his body between angry drivers and their animals, and arrested thousands of people over the years while onlookers gathered to watch a familiar show of street drama.

Sea

As I move to the sea as a site of theatre and the popular, I am indebted to a vibrant group of scholars in animal studies, performance studies, and environmental history—such as Adria Imada, *Aloha America* (2013); David Aiona Chang, *The World and All the Things Upon It* (2016); Jason M. Colby, *Orca* (2018); and Bathsheba Demuth, *Floating Coast* (2019). These texts are helping me to think critically about human and shark entanglements across history.[22] Popular culture, I contend, is where sharks are "made" in the popular imagination. Unprovoked shark attacks worldwide each year are far rarer than death by flying champagne cork.[23] Yet, because sharks are opportunistic feeders, they have shown up at some of the most traumatic scenes of human violence throughout history, including the Middle Passage, wars at sea, and colonial conquest. Moreover, the rise of physical culture and new oceanic economies of leisure in the late nineteenth century hastened human contact with sharks and other marine animals. In response to these historical locations of trauma and transformation, the "man-eating" shark occupies an outsize place in popular culture.

This last example focuses on the most famous pop-cultural shark vehicle ever made, the movie *Jaws*. Based on Peter Benchley's bestselling novel published in February 1974, *Jaws* was released on June 20, 1975. Debuting on the heels of the Watergate scandal and the nation's final evacuation from Vietnam, *Jaws* was an instant smash hit in a jittery nation. The film created a new cinematic category: the summer blockbuster. Directed by a virtually unknown twenty-eight-year-old named Steven Spielberg, *Jaws* grossed $60 million in its first month and soon became the first film to earn $100 million (based on studio profits after theatres collected their exhibition fees).[24] When released abroad, the film soon became a global sensation. Universal Pictures saturated the marketplace with *Jaws*-related consumer products: Americans bought *Jaws* T-shirts, foam shark fins, shark's-tooth pendants, "jawberry" ice cream, posters, and beach towels. *Jaws* terrified its audiences so completely that coastal tourist towns suffered economically. Frantic beachgoers panicked at the slightest provocation—whether it be a flock of ducks or a hapless baby whale dragged to shore and beaten. In this panicky milieu, frenzied swimmers occasionally became mobs. On June 23, 1975, *Time* magazine's cover headline was "Super Shark: *Jaws* on Film and Other Summer Thrillers." On July 28, 1975, *Newsweek* dubbed this national hysteria "Jawsmania."

Nonetheless, the film's path to blockbuster status was bumpy and by no means preordained. The movie's producers at Universal Pictures, David Brown and Richard Zanuck, possessed little scientific knowledge about sharks. Their ignorance ultimately determined the film's structure, content, and filming location. They initially assumed that they could use a trained great white shark in the film. According to screenwriter Carl Gottlieb, the producers wanted to hire a shark trainer, "who, with enough money, could get a great white shark to perform a few simple stunts on cue in long shots with a dummy in the water, after which they could cut to the miniatures or something for the close-up stuff."[25]

Peter Benchley quickly corrected the producers, whose assumptions conflated "killer whales"—*Cetacean* members of the dolphin family, *Delphinidae*—with "killer sharks." Orcas had been trained to perform in captivity at the new marine park SeaWorld since 1964, which strongly shaped the common misperception that sharks, too, could be trained.[26] The popular television show *Flipper* (1964–1967) heightened such misperceptions, as did the Depression-era bottlenose dolphin shows at Florida's Marine Studios designed by filmmaker and naturalist William Douglas Burden, who was involved in a shark repellent project with the US Navy during World War II. Cold War marine mammal weaponization programs such as the navy's Marine Mammal Program, founded in 1959, also contributed to popular mythologies of potentially trainable sharks.

Brown and Zanuck conquered the biological limits of the great white shark by commissioning the construction of four fake sharks. Like other material sources, these mechanical great whites offer their own biological and cultural insights into the history of human and shark entanglements. The mold for the *Jaws* sharks measured twenty-five feet long, twelve-and-a-half feet wide, and eight feet high.[27] Hidden behind a smooth fiberglass exterior and gaping toothy maw, a network of springs and gears facilitated movement. The mechanical sharks (each named "Bruce" after Steven Spielberg's lawyer) unwittingly dictated the film's location on a coast with a smooth, shallow, sandy bottom so that the film crews could operate the cranes, platforms, and catapults needed to animate the fake shark. Primarily for this reason, Martha's Vineyard was chosen. Nonetheless, the three fakes actually used in the first film broke down so often in the salt water that filming delays and major cost overruns were endemic. Director Steven Spielberg jokingly referred to these relentless production hiccups as "his Vietnam."[28] Yet the mechanical glitches ultimately proved serendipitous in the finished movie. The shark was rarely seen, and its absence made it far more suspenseful, frightening, and real—its spectral presence signaled by John Williams's two-note heartbeat soundtrack.[29]

Jaws heralded a new cinematic phenomenon in the summer of 1975: the summer "blockbuster," breaking every box office record until *Star Wars* was released two years later.[30] Clark Ramsay, director of advertising and public relations for Universal, compared "Sharkmania" to Beatlemania, "except that the Beatles' popularity was largely concentrated in a particular age group, while sharkmania seems to know no bounds."[31] The movie's ecological consequences were equally profound. The movie's prolonged shark hunt in its second half fueled an escalation of the "monster fishing" that Montauk, Long Island, fisherman Frank Mundus had popularized during the early 1950s. Participation in tournament shark fishing expeditions and commercial shark fishing outfits skyrocketed to the point that marine biologists noted a decline in US Atlantic shark populations. In a culture historically primed to loathe sharks as dangerous scavengers, the movie catalyzed a new generation of leisure killing.

After production finished on *Jaws*, workers hauled the three original fake sharks back to California and dumped them in a back lot at Universal Pictures, where they simply "rotted away" (according to their creator, production designer Joe Alves).[32] Nonetheless, the fakes helped create an enduring cultural phenomenon: the kitsch shark. In 1977, for example, the Peralvars Brothers Circus from Mexico staged a fake *Jaws*-inspired shark act at the end of the show, complete with a deep pool containing hundreds of gallons of water and a huge vinyl *tiburon* prowling and attacking performers in the water.[33] That same year, an episode of *Happy Days* featured Arthur "Fonzie" Fonzarelli, clad in his trademark leather jacket, improbably jumping over a circling dorsal fin on water skis. Decades later, this campy episode inspired a new phrase to describe a television show past its prime: It has "jumped the shark." More recently, the self-reflexively bad *Sharknado* series features fake sharks sucked into a tornado; the most recent (as of this writing) in this franchise, *Sharknado 6—The Last Sharknado, It's About Time*, was released in August 2018. The infectiously catchy K-pop sensation "Baby Shark" by Pinkfong is one of YouTube's most popular videos, with several billion views.[34] Even scientific organizations such as the marine tracking organization OCEARCH participate in this kitschy pop cultural shark frenzy.

When tagged sharks (such as the great white "Katharine" or the blue shark "CubsWin") surface, they ping a satellite tracking their movements, which sends notifications to their thousands of followers on Twitter and Facebook.[35] Here in Austin in pre-pandemic times, "*Jaws* on the Water" offered moviegoers an evening of fun and fear—watching the movie on a giant screen while floating in the water with divers lurking and pulling unsuspecting audience members off of their inner tubes. At Universal Studios Japan, a frightening *Jaws* boat ride through a facsimile Amity features a huge mechanical great white periodically popping out of the water.

And yet, this profusion of pop cultural sharks reveals a paradox: As sharks become even more visible in myriad iterations of theatre and the popular, their actual numbers are declining precipitously owing to a deadly combination of overfishing and bycatch; warming seas and climate change; plastic pellet ingestion; and shark finning, which alone kills an estimated one hundred million sharks per year. On January 28, 2021, the *New York Times* published the grim findings of a study in the journal *Nature*, which analyzes how more than three quarters of oceanic shark and ray species are threatened with extinction, in an article titled "Overfishing Has Put Rays and Sharks at Grave Risk."[36] While local populations of sharks off the US Atlantic and Pacific coasts remain healthy owing to effective federal regulations, the global decline of an order of animals that have survived five major extinctions over the past four hundred million years should be a call to action in the age of the Anthropocene.

Notes

1. See Stuart Hall, "Note on Deconstructing 'the Popular,'" in *People's History and Socialist Theory*, ed. Raphael Samuel (London: Routledge & Kegan Paul, 1981).

2. Raymond Williams, *Marxism and Literature* (New York: Oxford University Press, 1977), 11.

3. Robin D. G. Kelley, *Race Rebels: Culture, Politics, and the Black Working Class* (New York: Free Press, 1994), 57.

4. Sanjoy Hazarika, "Age-Old Hindu Barrier Falls: Women Are Priests," *New York Times*, July 3, 1984, A2.

5. Edward Said, *Orientalism* (New York: Verso, 1978).

6. Arlie Russell Hochschild, *The Managed Heart: Commercialization of Human Feeling* (Berkeley: University of California Press, 1985).

7. See Janet M. Davis, *The Circus Age: American Culture and Society Under the Big Top* (Chapel Hill: University of North Carolina Press, 2002).

8. Davis, *The Circus Age*; Gregory J. Renoff, *The Big Tent: The Traveling Circus in Georgia, 1820–1930* (Athens: University of Georgia Press, 2008).

9. Janet M. Davis, "The Circus Americanized," in *The American Circus*, ed. Susan Weber, Kenneth L. Ames, and Matthew Wittmann (New York and New Haven: Bard Graduate Center and Yale University Press, 2012), 48.

10. "Circus Day: Our Big Store Your Headquarters" advertisement, *Barton County Democrat* (Great Bend, KS), September 29, 1899, *Chronicling America: Historic American Newspapers*, LOC.

11. Emily Dickinson, "Poems, Second Series, XVIII," *Collected Poems*, quoted in Davis, *The Circus Age*, 28.

12. Sakina Mariam Hughes, "Under One Big Tent: American Indians, African Americans and the Circus World of Nineteenth-Century America," PhD dissertation, Michigan State University, 2012.

13. See Renoff, *The Big Tent*, 111; Davis, *The Circus Age*, 32–34.

14. "Move to Punish Duluth Lynchers," *New York Times*, June 17, 1920, ProQuest Historical Newspapers.

15. For a full account of the Duluth circus lynching, see Davis, "The Circus Americanized," 49–50.

16. For additional material on Bergh's life, see Ernest Freeberg, *A Traitor to His Species: Henry Bergh and the Birth of the Animal Rights Movement* (New York: Basic Books, 2020).

17. Russia was an enduring exotic other in nineteenth- and twentieth-century American social thought and popular culture; "Darkest Russia: A Grand Romance of the Czar's Realm" debuted as a popular theatrical melodrama in 1894 and film in 1917. Reference to "Darkest Russia" courtesy of Julia Mickenberg.

18. Bergh, quoted in Sidney H. Coleman, *Humane Society Leaders in America: With a Sketch of the Early History of the Humane Movement in England* (Albany, NY: American Humane Association 1924), 35–36. See also Freeberg, *A Traitor to His Species*; Clara Morris, "Riddle of the Nineteenth Century: Mr. Henry Bergh," *McClure's Magazine*, March 1902, 422.

19. NY Rev. Stat. tit. 6, sec. 26 (1829), in Animal Legal and Historical Center (website).

20. Coleman, *Humane Society Leaders in America*, 38.

21. C. C. Buel, "Henry Bergh and His Work," *Scribner's Monthly*, April 1879, 872–84, 872.

22. Adria Imada, *Aloha America: Hula Circuits through the U.S. Empire* (Durham, NC: Duke University Press, 2012); David A. Chang, *The World and All the Things Upon It* (Minneapolis: University of Minnesota Press, 2016); Jason M. Colby, *Orca: How We Came to Know and Love the Ocean's Greatest Predator* (New York: Oxford University Press, 2018); Bathsheba Demuth, *Floating Coast: An Environmental History of the Bering Strait* (New York: W. W. Norton, 2019).

23. "Annual Risk of Death During One's Lifetime: 18 Things More Likely

to Kill You than Sharks," International Shark Attack File, Florida Museum (website).

24. Rob Dimery, "1975: First Film to Reach $100 Million at the Box Office," August 19, 2015, *Guinness World Records* (website).

25. Carl Gottlieb, *The Jaws Log* (New York: Dell Publishing, 1975), 33.

26. On the history of Orca shows, see Susan G. Davis, *Spectacular Nature: Corporate Culture and the Sea World Experience* (Berkeley: University of California Press, 1997); Jane Desmond, *Staging Tourism: Bodies on Display from Waikiki to Sea World* (Chicago: University of Chicago Press, 2001).

27. Cory Turner, "From Junkyard to Museum: The Journey of a 'Jaws' Shark," February 10, 2016, *All Things Considered* on NPR (website).

28. Peter Schorsch, "35 Years Ago Today, 'Jaws' Was Unleashed on the World," June 21, 2010, *SaintPetersBlog* (blog).

29. For a definitive account of the production of the movie, see Carl Gottlieb, *The Jaws Log* (New York: Dell Publishing, 1975).

30. Peter Goldman and Martin Kasindorf, "Jawsmania: The Great Escape," *Newsweek*, July 28, 1975.

31. John Getze, "Jaws Swims to Top in Ocean of Publicity: Huge Film Promotion Began Before Book Was Published," *Los Angeles Times*, September 28, 1975, G1, ProQuest Historical Newspapers.

32. Owing to the movie's success, a fourth fake shark was commissioned from the original mold. But it was never used in subsequent films and thus was sold to a junkyard, whose owner preserved the hulking fake to advertise his business. The fake was restored and will now spend its remaining days in the new museum of the Academy of Motion Picture Arts and Sciences. Turner, "From Junkyard to Museum: The Journey of a 'Jaws' Shark."

33. Tim Tegge, update posted on Facebook, December 14, 2018.

34. Sonja Haller, "'Baby Shark' Doo Doo Doo'd Itself to No. 32 on the Billboard Hot 100," *USA Today* (website), January 10, 2019.

35. See individual shark profiles and movement data at the OCEARCH Shark Tracker, OCEARCH (website), accessed September 21, 2023.

36. Catrin Einhorn, "Overfishing Has Put Rays and Sharks at Grave Risk," *New York Times*, January 28, 2021, A23.

Unpopular Populism

Project 400 Theater's LES Travesti

Tom Fish

IN JULY 2000, burlesque performer and journalist of the downtown scene Trav S.D. boasted of the adventurous theatrical spirit bursting within New York City's Lower East Side (LES), featuring "Grade-Z budgets, Grade-A aspirations, and above all a desire to please the audience."[1] Working exclusively without external funding, the artists featured a trademark ingenuity necessitated by shoestring budgets. Most performed out of a collection of tiny storefront theatres operated by downtown maven Aaron Beall, scattered within a short radius of Stanton and Ludlow Streets. Trav S.D. champions the gritty artists as "theatrical populists."[2]

Project 400 Theater (1997–2005), a key player in the LES scene, developed a signature style of neo-travesti—a playful, often immersive burlesque of canonical works set to the soundtrack of American popular music with a penchant for targeting Shakespeare. Their company's four core performers, partly in homage to Charles Ludlam, developed a drag-clowning style but of an all-female-presenting variety. The company's name stood for their lofty aspirations: a dream to one day produce four hundred projects. Yet during their active years in NYC, that number was closer to thirty. Today, the company is largely remembered for their breakout commercial success, *The Donkey Show*, a raucous adaptation of *A Midsummer Night's Dream* told solely through the lyrics of disco anthems in a site-specific nightclub space modeled after Studio 54. The production began with humble starts, first mounted in a tiny, jewel-shaped speakeasy on Ludlow, hidden in the back of a retail business, the Piano Store. The production would gain enough momentum to run for more than seven years in NYC, expanding its reach with multiple international tours (Edinburgh, Madrid, Evian, London, Seoul). Company cofounder and Tony Award–winning director Diane Paulus was able to leverage its notability to help launch her solo-directorial career. Years later, Paulus remains a self-described "proud populist," albeit one who has now hit the quintessential big time.[3]

Project 400's scrappy, resourceful model of LES theatrical populism ultimately consolidated behind Paulus as its rising figurehead. By 2006, the company had become what actress and company member Emily Hellstrom describes as "The Diane Paulus Show," and it was clear to Hellstrom that "she didn't want to bring us with her." Under Paulus's reign, productions like *The Donkey Show* were no longer community-based endeavors and were increasingly subject to the commercial pressures of larger production budgets. This essay heralds Project 400's theatrical "unpopular populism" and how it functioned as a small-time mode of political critique. Theoretically, it borrows from Jack Halberstam's queer- and Marxist-inspired charge in *The Queer Art of Failure* to recuperate goofy archives.[4] Failure presents an often untapped, surprising source of strategies to reframe the meaning of success. Within this context, this essay playfully chooses to revel in a quartet of cross-gendering clowns to redefine how we identify, even value, the merits of theatrical populism. Ultimately, it suggests how theatre scholars can play a role in revealing bygone populist models, even shifting the models that we privilege toward the more grassroots and community affirming.

My approach follows what Jim McGuigan defines as a "critical cultural populism" that interrogates the relationship between contemporary political and economic formations and popular culture while also examining the possibility of a democratic populism or community renewal. By distinguishing a "small-time" populism, I look to mark a critical difference. As Dieter Lesage suggests in the *Populism Reader*, every "project on populism should claim as a basic right the right to use the term in different ways" but also should "enact difference. It should differ from itself."[5] Here, I explore populism as codified in particular theatrical events, rather than from a performance studies perspective more broadly. My focus on theatre as populist vehicle is supported by Ben Fink and Janelle Reinelt, who each look to identify and highlight theatre's progressive potential. Fink has detailed the impact and democratic vision of activist theatre in Appalachian coal mine country, and Reinelt has envisioned the potential of a left-wing populist theatre, modeled after Black Lives Matter.[6] Although Project 400 doesn't present a conscientiously political model like these, it offers a way to mine for progressive grassroots strategies amid commercial pressures.

Highs and Lows of Theatrical Populism

The Donkey Show's earlier and later incarnations represent contrasting models of theatrical populism, satisfying Lesage's recommendation to "use the term in different ways."[7] My interest in the subject stems from when I attended the production at El Flamingo in Chelsea, in spring 2001, an experience I found highly influential as a young theatre undergrad. It provided a jubilance and hands-on interaction that I had not yet experienced in a theatrical exchange. Years later, after Project 400 Theater dissolved, Paulus revived the production for her inaugural season as the artistic director at the American Repertory

Theater (ART) in Cambridge, Massachusetts, where it went on to run for a decade (2009–2019).

I auditioned and joined ART's debut cast as one of Titania's glittery, disco-clad go-go fairies (2009–2010). I would, however, come to discover a populist performance firmly entrenched in a mechanics of commercial reproduction. The rehearsal process itself was largely governed by NYC performance tapes in an effort to re-create earlier Project 400 efforts. This process was supplemented by frequent coaching sessions with previous cast members, who would visit from New York City to train us on characterization, movement, and improvisational play. ART's nontraditional performance space, called Oberon after the king of the fairies from Shakespeare's *A Midsummer Night's Dream*, was styled as a nightclub and allowed a fairly similar re-creation. Although produced as nonprofit theatre, the space and style of the event helped to satisfy commercial demands, in part through maximizing bar sales but also because the cabaret-style venue was not governed by Actors' Equity Association regulations and its pay scale. From my firsthand experience, the process felt surprisingly recycled, particularly in contrast to its carefree, carnivalesque spirit.

The Cambridge ART production sets up a contrast with Project 400's earlier incarnations. It highlights a commercial populist theatre model. Situated within a nonprofit landscape, the Cambridge *Donkey Show* suggested populism as a dubious claim, a performative rallying cry and marketing tactic used effectively to galvanize audiences. Its sense of community, moreover, was intricately manufactured. Nicholas Ridout and Erin Hurley have described commercial theatre's function as a virtual affect machine, soliciting feeling as a central commodity of exchange as part of bourgeois entertainment.[8] Being "of the people" was a sensation, a pleasurable feeling solicited though an assortment of affective labors. The production would employ tactics to arouse pleasurable affective engagement and a communal warmth for the audience/clubgoers, from the swirling disco ball to an explosion of papier-mâché butterflies falling from the sky.

One key example of these affective labors, orchestrated by the cast, was production's "preshow," a series of improvisational exchanges that began the event. Paulus directed us to create improvisational connections with audience members, referred to by production as "touching." At times figurative, at times literal, cast members may offer a flirtatious wink, a playful swipe with a glittered hand, or in the grandest incarnation: a disco gyration with a cast member atop a dance floor box (Figure 2.1). These moments, a hallmark of Project 400's craft, offered a sensation of pleasurable involvement, of playing a role in creating the quality "*of* the people." Paulus would frequently assert during rehearsals, in reference to Warhol's famous comment about Studio 54, that we were producing a "democracy on the dancefloor." And while we would effectively comingle nightly with various types—from a Harvard provost to bachelorette parties—such "democracy" equated to the widespread congeniality that our affective labors carefully maintained (figure 2.2). The antics of "touching" offered a sense of connection but also served as a tool of audience management within the nontraditional forum. By establishing familiarity with the crowd early on, the cast could more easily and quickly maneuver through a nightclub floor filled with drunken patrons.

Figure 2.1. Kingpin club owner Oberon welcomes clubgoers on the streets before the official start of the show, American Repertory Theater, Cambridge. Photo by Marcus Stern.

Figure 2.2. View of the dance floor during the preshow, American Repertory Theater, Cambridge. Photo by Marcus Stern.

Unlike the popular theatre Trav S.D. heralded a decade earlier, the production served as a big-time populist vehicle. Its debut was met with excitement but also reservation by some ART stakeholders. Many derided its overly commercial tactics, suggesting the production had "forsaken the ART in attempts to save it," was an "exploitation, not reinvention of Shakespeare," or simply was "pandering to sexual appetite." Paulus would remain steadfast that populism "doesn't mean a dumbing down of the theater" but presented a vehicle "giving the audience a voice." Michael Bristol offers a useful way to distinguish between the political work of Project 400's earlier and later versions, even though at face value they may appear to be replicas. He examines the role of "big-time Shakespeare," the pervasive capitalist influence shaping commercial appropriations, in a model borrowed from Mikael Bakhtin's notion of the "great time" of the *longue durée*. In response, Christy Desmet has acknowledged the significant political and cultural work afforded to a complementary, "small-time" Shakespeare, which represents a more progressive community-based model of appropriation.[9]

Project 400's style of pop music adaptation and their ability to "touch" audiences remained virtually the same in NYC, Cambridge, and abroad. Where the big-time theatrical populism focused on manufacturing a pleasurable sense of community and connectivity as part of its commercial appeal, the small-time used the fabric of community and resourceful carnivalesque techniques as a mechanism for both survival and community-based renewal.

Toward an Unpopular Populism

Project 400 embodied its own spirit of community-based renewal founded upon clever recycling. The artistic climate resulted from a dearth of financial support, with limited audience sizes in LES and a lack of institutionalized funding. Their economic and creative independence, as alluded to in the opening, became a badge of honor to LES theatre makers, who also generally failed to attract or employ outside producers. Hillary Miller's scholarship on the economy of NYC theatre would also trace the financial challenges to the "regimes of scarcity" that reshaped downtown theatre in response to the 1970s financial crisis, with lasting results.[10] *The Donkey Show* was performed hundreds of times in downtown Manhattan but, as company member Murdy describes, "exclusively in stolen spaces."[11] On Ludlow Street, they performed in the back of the Piano Store in a speakeasy that, according to urban legend, was fully functioning during Prohibition. The theatrical space, precariously tucked away, contained its own residue of historical rule breaking. For the burlesque troupe, playing fast and loose with the Bard, the pairing was kismet. The complete name for the debut production was *I Love Lucifer, Part One: The Donkey Show*, suggesting its devious, yet cheeky intentions. The premiere featured the *Midsummer* lovers as Lucy, Ricky, Fred, and Ethel, lending itself to the title's pun off the classic sitcom. Their raucous performances challenged Shakespearean authority by eschewing every word of heightened language, privileging pop lyrics, improvisational banter, and the playful antics of an array of puppets. (The puppets and *I Love Lucy* characters would be dropped in a later iteration and the title of the show abridged.)[12]

The site-specific gender-crossing performances could function as what Elizabeth Freeman calls *temporal* drag, tapping into bygone historical moments and "cultural castoffs" for revolutionary potential and revitalization.[13] Freeman's concept develops from a broader theoretical movement that is central to the methodology of this argument and frequently referred to as queer theory's temporal turn. From the early 2000s, amid the celebrations of new advances in the gay rights movement, it became alarmingly clear to queer scholars that benefits were accruing disproportionately to a certain class of LGBT citizens that Lisa Duggan has termed "homonormative." Subsequently, queerness became redefined as embodied forms of sexual and gender expression that challenge progressive temporal regimes, what Freeman calls "chrononormativity" or José Esteban Muñoz terms "straight time."[14] The focal point for this theoretical movement became mining for embodied ways to challenge the temporal logic embedded in linear, reproductive economies, both commercial and sexual. Freeman's notion of temporal drag, for instance, suggests reclaiming failures of the past—as in "what a *drag*!"—then converting them to into a creative spark, a political repurposing and renewal. Relatedly, Halberstam's model, adapted from Gramsci's "low theory," explores how popular culture is inevitably driven by prevailing commercial and heteronormative standards of success. Consequently, he encourages scholars in an unconventional, perhaps counterintuitive, way to uncover silly "low" archives in order to reveal surprising models of connectivity. These models intrinsically go against the commercial grain, forged outside of heteronormative standards of reproductivity. For scholars, they can serve as clandestine modes of community-building produced through failure but worth celebrating.

The LES in the 1990s was a hotbed of creative resistance to uptown consumerism but was itself destined to fail. In the 2000s, many of the vibrant theatre companies would fold under rising economic pressures, particularly amid skyrocketing real estate prices. The area also became a hot spot of nightlife tourism, drawing uptown crowds. The Piano Store, home to the disco *Midsummer* and a slew of other Project 400 experiments, would be converted from a theatre into a full-time restaurant/live music venue. With it went creative landmarks like the nearby "Gas Station," a derelict gas station repurposed in the 1980s into a postapocalyptic, open-air exhibition and performance space. By the late 1990s, its metallic sculpture garden, a shrine to low art, had been replaced by a Duane Reade.

Revisiting Project 400's small-time clownish travesti and its traces of a bygone theatrical populism may act as its own mode of historical recuperation. It suggests how grassroots theatrical populism, often overcome by commercial pressures, may surface a treasure trove of horizontal strategies and relational tactics that value connectivity over commerce.

LES Travesti

The remainder of the essay highlights some of Project 400's creative tactics of community-based appropriation, strategies necessitated by economic challenges that firmly rooted the theatre of "the people" and the downtown scene. Most notable would be the integration of popular music, which was a hallmark of every one of their dozens of shows. Cofounders Paulus and Weiner first discovered the value of popular music during summer theatre experimentation in Door County, Wisconsin, in the early-to-mid-1990s. Their company, then called Blue Circle, convinced a local R&B biker bar band to write and perform original music for their *Tempest* adaptation, *Prospero's Revenge* (1993). The music foregrounded their popular theatre style that, according to Weiner, was principally about "driving the audiences" not in an intellectual way but through "connecting to people's emotions . . . on a visceral level."[15] A strategic hierarchical inversion was employed as pop music, and its reverberations created affective responses, privileging a bodily "lower" stratum over the "high" and cerebral.

Pop music served as a primary means to foreground audiences. Paulus highlights how in the American tradition, popular music is such because "the people" have demanded it, which she contrasts with a European subsidized cultural tradition. In *The Donkey Show*, and most of their productions, performers would sing along with the pop music tracks, with their original, recognizable vocals still prominently featured. The approach would convert the theatrical event into a pop ritual, building off sing-along traditions from the bar, karaoke club, and even the car.[16] The practice encouraged all participants, the cast and attendees, to take part in a communal moment of reverence to the pop anthem and its historical moment. The licensed songs would mark more than sing-along tracks, since they doubled as the actual dialogue for the performance, centralizing the popular within the Shakespearean storyline. The music also activated the conventions of the nightclub, casting the audience as clubgoers instead of theatregoers and creating an affectively arousing popular event that engaged the audience's full sensorium.

By performing almost exclusively in clubs, which were nontraditional theatre spaces, the company followed an off-off Broadway tradition dating to the 1960s. As Steven Bottoms details, much downtown theatrical playing was done in alternative spaces such as "cafes, churches, basements, and lofts." The lineage of NYC underground theatre further influenced Project 400's performance style. Beyond borrowing liberally from the playbook of the Theatre of the Ridiculous, combining burlesque with cross-gender performance, their audience participation was modeled after that of Artaud. The company's immersive elements were an extension of his ritualistic "holy theatre," but lacking the countercultural "radically anticonsumerist vision" common to their predecessors.[17] Although Project 400 drew upon downtown legacies of the avant-garde, their populist style ironically served as an indictment of these very practices. The cofounders, Weiner and Paulus, believed that the most "popular" downtown theatre of the 1980s generally ignored the interests—and even enjoyment—of their audiences. Weiner describes a much-anticipated revival of Martha Graham's *Every Soul Is a Circus* (1986) as tantamount to a theatrical buzzkill: dull and stripped of all the playful engagement and vibrancy of an *actual* circus. They found this trend all too common, inspiring them to challenge a "solipsistic theater world" by employing recognizable music and theatrical immersion.[18]

The company's trademark nightclub theatre allowed them to graft the local community into the fabric of production. Not only did they use "stolen spaces," but Murdy characterizes the troupe's appropriations of found spaces as "always trespassing.". Their annual LES *Community Show* in 2001 appeared quite literally on a corner on Stanton Street. Described at once as "celebratory block party and environmental theatre," the event kicked off the newly founded annual New York Fringe Festival, spearheaded by Beall and local artists.[19] It boasted of musicians on rooftops, actors on fire escapes, and Tennessee Williams's *Camino Real* as adapted source text. Site-specific performance became central to their small-time populist aesthetic. The company invented a karaoke club *Comedy of Errors* (2003–2005) and even workshopped a wrestling ring WWF *Lohengrin* set to a soundtrack of opera favorites from Verdi to Puccini.

Notably, in 2000, they collaborated on a strip club *Measure for Measure*, which played at the notorious Show World Center at Eighth Avenue and Forty-Second Street. The space marked one of NYC's longest-running adult entertainment venues, yet due to Giuliani's 1990s Disneyfication efforts in Times Square, it faced foreclosure. Under the mayor's infamous 60/40 law, 60 percent of the business products couldn't be of the erotic variety. Beall developed Nada Show World, a midtown branch of Nada Theater, featuring strip club–themed theatrical entertainments in the empty cabaret stage (no actual nudity was allowed). Paulus found Show World to be the perfect corollary for Shakespeare's play about a tyrant cracking down ruthlessly on the city's sexual immorality. The play's title, *Show World Reunion Tour*, indicates the basic premise, which converted the play into an interactive event, including the ability to buy a (fully clothed) lap dance. Audiences would arrive at a one-night-only reunion to celebrate the glory days of the now bygone adult entertainment venue, with the strippers' debut call to the stage to Mötley Crüe's "Girls, Girls, Girls." The performance was also structured as an explicit populist critique of authority. As former owner Tony, played by Murdy, tells the crowd at the production's opening, Show World "closed almost two years ago—a victim of Mr. Giuliani's crackdown on a *certain segment* of the entertainment industry."[20] In a strategic high/low inversion, the characters turned to Shakespeare, since "we have to present something that's a little more legitimate."[21] Audiences played a crucial role in creating the live atmosphere of the event. Concurrently, they assumed an active part in the celebration and recuperation of a failing Show World institution in the face of big-time economic pressures.

The production's unapologetic reverence for sensuous bodies featured an additional hierarchical inversion. The conscientious focus on nether regions embodied a playful—and sometimes literal—bottoms-up carnivalesque. In *Show World*, this was often of a goofy variety; the visibly pregnant Juliet character, for example, would lap milk out of a bowl while earnestly pretending to be a cat. *The Donkey Show* also featured a number of scantily clad performers. Set within an immersive environment, their comfort and even pride in their bodies could serve as an invitation to audiences (figure 2.3). As Paulus describes, "it tells everyone there, you can feel good too. . . . It's ok, you can be whoever you are." Concurrently, this was foregrounded by disco. Richard Dyer details how the music's structure and rhythms solicit "expressive, sinuous movement" that "restores eroticism to the whole of the body."[22]

The disco *Midsummer* would expand its sensuous engagements to the gritty streets around Stanton. Nightly, Oberon and Titania began the performance from the Pink Pony, a late-night coffee joint, then reenacted the opening fairy king and queen's fight as an improvised feud traveling all the way down the LES. Project 400 member and company actress Anna Wilson, adorned with a lavish cape, knee-high heeled boots, and butterfly pasties, recalls decades later how, when she played Titania, she would angrily kick and "there was so much trash, so much crap, it would fly through the air." The prelude became its own spectacle, often stopping traffic. The exuberant kicks Wilson fondly recalls converted waste into vibrant storytelling. LES, at the time, was synonymous with refuse. *Donkey Show* performer Jordin Ruderman describes: "It was like completely rat infested. We would, I mean seriously we were in the bathroom changing and there'd be like roach running over our feet. I mean, it was not pretty or fancy NY at all. It was down and dirty and we were down and dirty and we loved it."[23] For small-time theatrical populists, recuperating LES filth was a visceral connection to the street. It embodied a characteristically downtown creative inversion, a playful liberation from the—often more cerebral—uptown artists.

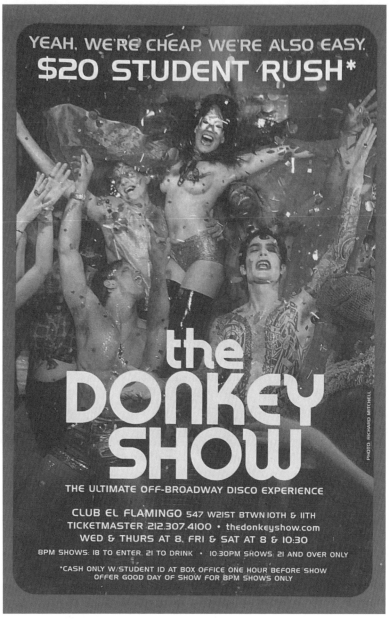

Figure 2.3. Marketing flyer highlights Project 400's immersive, visceral, even sensual aesthetic, Club El Flamingo. Photo: richardmitchell.com

Relatedly, the process of community-based renewal was firmly entrenched in the company's costuming practices, which relied almost exclusively on scouring secondhand stores. Out of economic necessity, each of the actresses spent countless hours for each production delving into vintage clothing archives. Murdy describes how the clothing would make "the man," it was "like a character, hanging in my closet." Similarly, Hellstrom presented each clothing item as a means of how "characters were born" via a treasure hunt that resulted, in her case, in "finding [her] own shoes." The thrift store became an archive of downtown histories, with objects carrying LES traces. The performers could activate a dormant past through a celebratory renewal. Murdy enthusiastically details "one of [her] proudest moments as a character actress." While working on *Show World*, she discovered the club had an extra original vest from the 1970s that "sort of . . . maybe a little . . . *touched* a doorman at the peep show." During the preshow, disguised in drag, she would act as a barker at the entrance, where they "still have the original 70s décor, sleazy décor." She would pass out XXX flyers (refashioned as G-rated show advertisements), hollering crudely to passersby, "You looking for the peep show or for the Shakespeare?"[24] Through such moments in vintage male garb, Murdy embodied a temporal drag, reanimating Show World's forlorn past through playful parody and inviting others to join in the boisterous recuperation.

Performance on the streets outside the adult entertainment venue effectively advertised the show but also teased that this may be a more "hands on" variety of Shakespeare. Project 400's site-specific performances did lend themselves to active community engagement. Hellstrom details how moving *The Donkey Show* from the Piano Store to the Pyramid Club, just a few blocks north in the East Village, energized the play by infusing it with a gay male club culture. The bar was iconic as one of the first drag bars in NYC (a frequent stomping ground for a 1990s RuPaul Charles). Since the *Midsummer* disco world was modeled after Studio 54, the iconic destination for late 1970s LGBT nightlife, Pyramid's queer culture could breathe life into the immersive performance space. Similarly, Ruderman relished how when the production later moved to El Flamingo in Chelsea, the fully staffed nightclub would "spontaneously take part in the theatrical illusion . . . calling the players by character names and getting shout outs during the show." For the performers, this added a richness to the immersive theatrical illusion, bolstering their own authority, since "all of a sudden, we had like the Mafia on our side."[25]

The four travesti performers were also bolstered by their trespassing within male space. As Laurence Senelick describes, female theatrical cross-dressing provides a means of empowerment, a "usurpation of male preserves."[26] In Project 400's theatrical worlds, the spaces themselves, traditionally owned and operated by men, would now be under the dominion of the female drag-clown figure (Figure 2.4). When *The Donkey Show* was performed at

El Flamingo, its club staff followed the lead of performers and referred to it exclusively as "Club Oberon" on performance nights. The king of the fairies, Oberon (played by Murdy), dressed as a 1970s kingpin, would both assert his authority and create a congenial environment through playful improvisations on the streets outside the club. His invitation and playful attire served as a gateway, insinuating to crowds that they were entering a place of play and a world where traditional hierarchies were suspended. The Vinnies (played by Hellstrom and Ruderman), a pair of fool characters from the Bronx, would find themselves not-cool-enough to get past the red rope. The pair would bargain, beg, and ultimately solicit multiple club patrons to try to get themselves in the door. Their creative antics to get inside became a twist on the classic "flop" clown act. Each attempt and subsequent failure would require more playful audience interaction as The Vinnies would carefully probe the line for women to recruit through amorous advances. Part of their clown persona was to be dumbstruck at the beauty and extravagance of *every* woman. As they flirted boisterously in the hope of sneaking inside, they would circulate what Sarah Warner describes as "acts of gaiety."[27] These strategies, central to the Project 400's politics of pleasure, served as jubilant, sometimes irreverent tactics for LGBTQ activism, ripe with gender upheaval and the possibility of homoerotic frisson.

Figure 2.4. To the surprise of the audience, the actress playing Mia dons Oberon's jacket and glasses to indicate that she played both roles. *The Donkey Show* curtain call, Club El Flamingo. Photo courtesy of Lauren Rubin

The Vinnies' flop act offered its own challenge to authority. David Peterson's study of contemporary clowning in Shakespeare draws upon Halberstam to establish how the flop "offers a new way to find success."[28] The duo would fail and try again and again, spreading their gaiety among clubgoers. Later, after the Vinnies have managed to sneak into the club, they reappear on the dance floor rebranded in new attire as Demetri and Helen. The flop act then resumes with new characters in different attire: drag king Demetri, the John Travolta of disco dancers, would use his swagger to seduce ladies throughout the crowd, as the doting Helen desperately tried to intervene. The unrequited lover would eagerly solicit men and women on the dance floor in a desperate attempt to make Demetri jealous. Just as he would target and make his move, Helen would propel herself (and often an innocent bystander) into interrupting the sensual transaction. The pattern would repeat, fail, then repeat again as the duo effectively worked their way "touching" one-by-one through the crowd in a model of recuperating failure first developed out of the LES community and its regenerative small-time aesthetic.

Conclusion

The story of *The Donkey Show* over the decades illustrates how theatrical populism can transform under commercial opportunity. As the nightclub venues grew to accommodate larger audiences, so did the spectacle. (In Cambridge and Miami, aerial artistry featured prominently.) Yet Project 400's mise-en-scène and style of audience engagement remained the same. As Paulus's inaugural ART production, it ushered in a new theatrical populism, subverting the company's long-standing commitment to avant-garde experimentation under previous artistic direction. With this, Paulus's fervent commitment to jolting Boston audiences through pop music and audience engagement channeled Project 400's early spirit of rebellion. Her appointment served as a mandate to expand ART's audience base through rousing, commercially viable popular theatre. Project 400's small-time theatrical populism was now Paulus's big-time one.

For the quartet of actresses who spent nearly a decade cultivating this joyous brand of downtown pop burlesque, the end was particularly bitter. Hellstrom describes how the company dissolved, and how this was never formally relayed to the actresses, who also failed to retain royalties on virtually all the productions they helped to create: "We were like a freak show, a carnival sideshow locked away in the closet."[29] Yet just as the clown flop sparks a promise of renewal, the untold story of Project 400—overshadowed, undervalued, and about 370 projects short of their goal—reveals a surprising treasure trove of strategies built from small-time community fibers. Their goofy, vintage archive can now serve as a small-time testament to the ironic merits and bygone pleasures of an unpopular populism.

Notes

1. Trav S.D., "'The Poseidon Adventure'—Coming to a Stage Near You!" *Village Voice* (website), July 25, 2000.

2. The term also became a self-description for some of the LES artists looking to articulate their brand of popular theatre, but this marks one of its early published references: Trav S.D., "'The Poseidon Adventure'—Coming to a Stage Near You!" *Village Voice* (website), July 25, 2000.

3. Patrick Healy, "High Art Meets High Jinks Onstage," *New York Times*, February 3, 2010, AR1.

4. Emily Hellstrom (company member and actor) in discussion with Tom Fish, October 2021; Jack Halberstam, *The Queer Art of Failure* (Durham, NC: Duke University Press, 2011).

5. Dieter Lesage, "Populism and Democracy," in *The Populism Reader*, ed. Cristina Ricupero, Lars Bang Larsen, and Nicolaus Schafhausen (Cambridge, MA: MIT Press, 2005), 12; and Jim McGuigan, *Cultural Populism* (New York: Routledge, 1992).

6. See Ben Fink, "Secular Communion in the Coalfield," *TDR* 64, no. 4 (2020): 16–43; and Janelle Reinelt, "Politics Populism Performance," *Performance Research* 24, no. 8 (2019): 59–68.

7. Dieter Lesage, "Populism and Democracy," in *The Populism Reader*, ed. Lars Bang Larsen, Cristina Ricupero, and Nicolaus Schafhausen (London: Lukas & Sternberg, 2005), 6.

8. See Nicholas Ridout, *Stage Frights, Animals, and Other Theatrical Problems* (Cambridge, UK: Cambridge University Press, 2006); and Erin Hurley, *Theatre & Feeling* (New York: Palgrave Macmillan, 2010), 4.

9. Joan Anderman, *Boston Magazine* 52, no. 2 (2014); Christopher Wallenberg, *American Theatre*, May 2011; Healy, "High Art Meets High Jinx Onstage." For politics of Shakespearean appropriation, see Michael Bristol, *Big-Time Shakespeare* (New York: Routledge, 1996) and the introduction to Christy Desmet and Robert Sawyer, eds., *Shakespeare and Appropriation* (London: Routledge, 1999), 1–14.

10. Hillary Miller, *Drop Dead: Performance in Crisis, 1970s New York* (Evanston, IL: Northwestern University Press, 2016), 1.

11. Rachel Murdy (company member and actor) in discussion with Fish, August 2021.

12. Randy Weiner, *I Love Lucifer: Part 1, The Donkey Show* (1998), unpublished manuscript in Fish's possession.

13. Rachel Murdy (company member and actor) in discussion with Fish, August 2021; also see Elizabeth Freeman, *Time Binds: Queer Temporalities, Queer Histories* (Durham, NC: Duke University Press, 2010), 68.

14. Lisa Duggan, *The Twilight of Equality? Neoliberalism, Cultural Politics,*

and the Attack on Democracy (Boston: Beacon House, 2003), 50; José Esteban Muñoz, *Cruising Utopia: The Then and There of Queer Futurity* (New York: New York University Press, 2009), 25.

15. Randy Weiner (playwright, company cofounder) in discussion with the Fish, September 2021.

16. Lenora Inez Brown, "She Turns the Beat Around," *American Theatre*, January 2002, 120; Eric Copage, "It's Not Your Mother's Musical, and That's the Point," *New York Times*, September 6, 1999.

17. Stephen Bottoms, *Playing Underground: A Critical History of the 1960s Off-Off-Broadway Movement* (Ann Arbor: University of Michigan Press, 2006), 2, 237.

18. On Graham production, Randy Weiner (playwright, company cofounder) in discussion with Fish, September 2021; Copage, "It's Not Your Mother's Musical, and That's the Point."

19. Simi Horwitz, "Community Show in Fringe Festival," *Backstage* (website), updated November 5, 2019.

20. Rachel Murdy (company member and actor) in discussion with Fish, August 2021.

21. Rachel Murdy (company member and actor) in discussion with Fish, August 2021; Adam Gopnik, "The Naked City," *New Yorker* 77, no. 20 (2001): 30–33; Randy Weiner, *The Show World Reunion Show* (2000), unpublished manuscript in Fish's possession.

22. Diane Paulus, interview by Jared Bowen, *Center Stage with Jared Bowen*, WGBH, October 8, 2009; Richard Dyer, "In Defense of Disco," *New Formations* 58 (Summer 2006): 105.

23. Anna Wilson (company member and actor) in discussion with Fish, August 2021; Jordin Ruderman (company member and actor) in discussion with Fish, September 2021.

24. Rachel Murdy (company member and actor) in discussion with Fish, August 2021.

25. Emily Hellstrom (company member and actor) in discussion with Fish, October 2021; Jordin Ruderman (company member and actor) in discussion with Fish, September 2021.

26. Laurence Senelick, *The Changing Room: Sex, Drag and Theatre* (London: Routledge, 2000).

27. Sara Warner, *Acts of Gaiety: LGBT Performance and the Politics of Pleasure* (Ann Arbor: University of Michigan Press, 2012), xv.

28. David Peterson, "Clowning on and Through Shakespeare" (doctoral dissertation, University of Pittsburgh, 2014), 31.

29. Emily Hellstrom (company member and actor) in discussion with Fish, October 2021.

Ndangered Narratives

Ernie McClintock as an Early Facilitator of Hip-Hop Theatre

Elizabeth M. Cizmar

IN ANTHOLOGIES ON the Black Theatre Movement, Ernie McClintock (1937–2003) appears in passing paragraphs and footnotes. In his forty-year career, the teacher and director established formidable theatre institutions, including the Afro-American Studio for Acting and Speech (est. 1966), the 127th Street Repertory Ensemble (est. 1973), and, in Richmond, the Jazz Actors Theatre (est. 1993). Within these institutions, he developed an acting technique eventually called Jazz Acting. In its early stages of development, Jazz Acting was known as the Theatre of Common Sense. Unlike mainstream acting methods, Jazz Acting departs from Stanislavski-based approaches in which, akin to its musical namesake, the script is considered a melody and the actors are musicians who riff in live performance. McClintock developed the technique to center on Black ontological experiences, an identifying component of Afrocentric acting methodology. McClintock's pupils applied their technique to scripted works like N. R. Davidson's *El Hajj Malik* and his all-Black casting of Peter Shaffer's *Equus*, both receiving rave reviews from the *New York Times*.

In addition to productions of published plays, Ernie McClintock also produced unscripted work with his students, who performed on the streets of New York City and Richmond, Virginia. I refer to these works as collectively authored pieces because the cast and McClintock, together, created the content for these theatrical events. In McClintock's process, the actors, as opposed to a playwright or a director, generated the material and structure and dictated the content. In the 1960s and 1970s, these theatrical events surrounded the political and social gestalt of the United States. By the time McClintock had moved to Richmond in the early 1990s, the collectively authored pieces in terms of content and form reflected what is now known as hip-hop theatre. This article argues that Ernie McClintock was an early facilitator of the popular genre, establishing his distinct Jazz Acting style of hip-hop theatre. His brand of hip-hop theatre is identified by the actors determining their sociopolitical concerns of the time and connecting with their immediate community. By focusing on the individual actors' voices as well as the company's collective push against the hegemony, McClintock's theatre inherently subverted Black stereotypes.

Initially, in the late 1960s and early 1970s in New York, the collectively authored piece *Where It's At* was performed on wagons that traveled from borough to borough. Each year, the show's theme would change as the actors chose topics related to their sociopolitical concerns. In a 1970 interview on New York Public Radio, McClintock stated the purpose of *Where It's At*: "I feel that certainly the kind of thing we are doing now comes out of the immediate experiences of the majority of the people we play for before, in the street."[1] This intention to reach popular audiences persisted throughout his career. Engaging with his community and making theatre accessible to the public was a critical part of his belief system. Through these theatrical events, McClintock's technique and directorial aesthetic extended to a versatile array of genres, styles, and presentations yet remained rooted in the Afrocentric notions of self-determination and community, centering the content on the direct lived experiences of Black Americans.

Marc Primus, McClintock's colleague and fellow founding figure of the Afro-American Studio for Acting and Speech, noted that McClintock was always interested in creating new work to address the urgent concerns of his company through his model of street theatre. In the early 1990s, according to Primus, McClintock "was interested in converting hip-hop to theatre."[2] McClintock's street theatre engaged with the community and worked against mainstream theatrical practices in form and content. These works were not typical plays with distinct characters and a cohesive narrative; rather, they were pieces of poetry, stories, music, and dance that gave voice to Black performers from varying experiences and backgrounds.

The roots of McClintock's hip-hop aesthetic can be traced from *Where It's At* to the Richmond theatre scene of the 1990s. In 2002, the year before McClintock passed, he, along with his ensemble members, produced two original hip-hop pieces, *The Rose That Grew from Concrete* and *Ndangered*. *Rose* is a collection of poems, songs, and stories by McClintock's mentee Tupac Shakur, who was murdered in 1996. *Ndangered* explores issues affecting young Black men in Richmond, such as Black masculinity, sexually transmitted infections, incarceration, and stereotypes. Via these collectively authored pieces created through the lens of McClintock's Jazz Acting aesthetic, his respective ensembles explored a multitude of Black perspectives, ultimately disrupting monolithic notions of Black identity.

The Hip-Hop Connection

McClintock's work is in conversation with hip-hop scholarship in terms of social justice, community engagement, and the concept of Nommo. According to director and scholar Daniel Banks, hip-hop theatre emerged in the 1990s, when British dancer/poet/emcee Jonzi D coined the term to describe a blended performance style.[3] Hip-hop developed as a form of political and social resistance by youth of color and their allies in urban centers across the United States. As Banks notes, hip-hop itself is much more than a musical genre; it is a multiethnic, grassroots, global culture leveraging self-expression to combat social justice. The theatrical genre was "born out of [a] struggle to own both content and form and, in that way, owes a direct debt to the activist and resistance culture of Hip Hop."[4] Nicole Hodges Persley, hip-hop theatre scholar, identifies elements of this popular genre, including nonlinearity and direct address to audiences, that break from conventional theatrical realism.[5] With this surge in scholarship, hip-hop theatre has become a popular theme for courses, festivals, conference panels, and youth camps.

Several aspects distinguish hip-hop theatre from other performance genres. The identifiable components of hip-hop theatre include community engagement, voicing youth's political and social concerns, challenging mainstream theatrical forms, reflecting popular culture, engaging with dialogue on class disparities, and telling stories of marginalized members of society who often are excluded from the mainstream stage.[6] In McClintock's hip-hop productions and his technique at large, community engagement was a necessary Afrocentric component. McClintock's purpose for founding a training ground for Black actors in 1966 was to establish a culturally specific institution and offer Afrocentric theatre as a way to speak to the Harlem community. Through McClintock's teaching and directing, *Where It's At*, *Ndangered*, and *The Rose That Grew from Concrete* challenged the status quo, a characteristic of hip-hop theatre identified by Hodges Persley.[7]

Another way McClintock connects to hip-hop is through the notion of Nommo, a spiritual concept from Mali that considers the human body and mind to be one with the force of life and intimately connected with the earth and the first ancestors. Nommo informs theatrical performance with an emphasis on vocality: "The power of the *word*, that Nommo force which manipulates all forms of raw life and conjures images that not only represent his biological place in Time and Space, but his spiritual existence as well."[8] As Banks notes, many hip-hop theatre practitioners were artistically raised on the concept of Nommo. McClintock provided space for Black youth to express their social and political concerns in a nonlinear story with a poetic vernacular.

Where It's At

McClintock's street theatre of the late 1960s and early 1970s prioritized the collective voice of the ensemble as well as the individual voices of the actors while breaking Eurocentric theatrical conventions. Due to the piece's popular appeal, *Where It's At* garnered attention from mainstream newspapers such as the *New York Times* and the Black publication the *New York Amsterdam News*. The actors created work in response to the politics of the 1960s under the theme of dissecting Blackness in America, echoing the underpinnings of Black Power. Each actor-writer's ontological experience and particular voice was welcome in creating and performing these pieces. Integrating the lived experiences and multitude of Black identities was a foundational component of the acting technique and rehearsal process. One can trace how McClintock's Street theatre served as a predecessor for hip-hop theatre.

McClintock's street theatre featured both the individual actor's response to their lived reality and audience engagement. These two concepts were a significant piece of the Jazz Acting technique and were effectively applied in collectively authored work. McClintock welcomed into his creation of this theatrical content the distinct experiences and nuanced identities of Black people, underlining the notion that the Black experience is not monolithic. In his theatre, Black Power, womanist, Afro-Caribbean, and queer points of views were equally important to the plight of Black liberation. A 1969 flyer for *Where It's At* (see figure 3.1) reads: "We guarantee a unique evening as we offer you a kaleidoscope of ourselves reacting to our environment in our own way. You are part of that environment."[9] With the image of a kaleidoscope, this show hearkens back to Paul Carter Harrison's description of the kaleidoscopic character of the African diaspora,[10] which McClintock embraced in cultivating Black actors from various backgrounds. Although each person's expression and experience varied, McClintock's students were all grappling with the fight for equality. In a 1970 interview, McClintock references the civil unrest in the country, then exacerbated by Richard Nixon's presidency. The US economy had stagnated, the nation's continued involvement in the Vietnam War propelled citizens to protest for peace, and many theatres closed because federal funding for the arts was slashed.[11] In productions like *Where It's At*, McClintock encouraged his students to bring their thoughts and opinions about America to this artistic process.

McClintock brought his troupe to the streets to perform unconventional pieces that acknowledged the stark contrast between an enclosed theatre and outdoor spaces. Theatre scholar Mance Williams's account of the Black Theatre Movement recognized how McClintock's early work cultivated the actor's craft in this context: "The actor must maintain the artistic standards of the production while responding to the reactions of the audience."[12] This principle connects to the Jazz Acting notion of riffing, in which performers respond

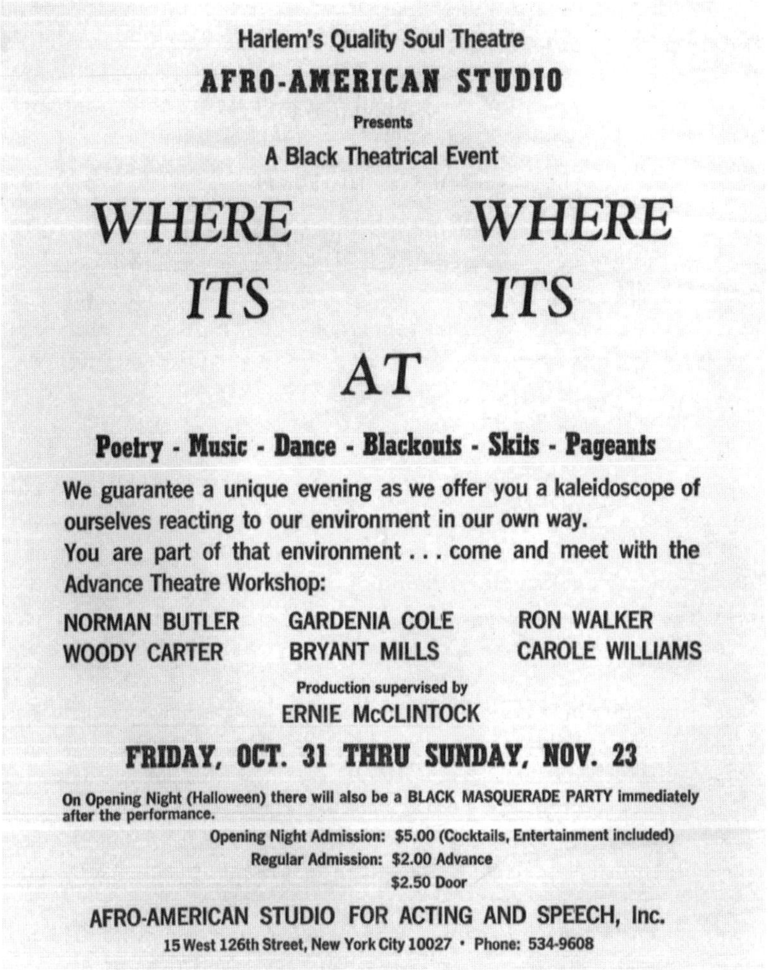

> Harlem's Quality Soul Theatre
> **AFRO-AMERICAN STUDIO**
> Presents
> A Black Theatrical Event
>
> # WHERE ITS WHERE ITS AT
>
> **Poetry - Music - Dance - Blackouts - Skits - Pageants**
>
> We guarantee a unique evening as we offer you a kaleidoscope of ourselves reacting to our environment in our own way.
> You are part of that environment... come and meet with the Advance Theatre Workshop:
>
> | | | |
> |---|---|---|
> | NORMAN BUTLER | GARDENIA COLE | RON WALKER |
> | WOODY CARTER | BRYANT MILLS | CAROLE WILLIAMS |
>
> Production supervised by
> **ERNIE McCLINTOCK**
>
> **FRIDAY, OCT. 31 THRU SUNDAY, NOV. 23**
>
> On Opening Night (Halloween) there will also be a BLACK MASQUERADE PARTY immediately after the performance.
> Opening Night Admission: $5.00 (Cocktails, Entertainment included)
> Regular Admission: $2.00 Advance
> $2.50 Door
>
> **AFRO-AMERICAN STUDIO FOR ACTING AND SPEECH, Inc.**
> 15 West 126th Street, New York City 10027 • Phone: 534-9608

Figure 3.1. Advertisement for Where It's At. Courtesy of the Private Collection of Geno Brantley.

to and build off of audience reactions, which vary from night to night. Such riffing requires actors to be fully present and responsive to the distinct makeup of the audience. The outcome is an immediate identification with strangers in unexpected circumstances and locations, such as the Bushwick neighborhood in Brooklyn, where spectators came out of their homes to listen from their stoops, set up chairs in front of the stage, or watched through their windows.[13] Certainly, audience reactions differed from neighborhood to neighborhood, and in the Bushwick performance, the primarily Latinx crowd of the 1970s did not enthusiastically respond to themes related to Black pride. But there were efforts to strip away the pretension often associated with theatre in the context of an exclusive space that separated the actors from the audience. Ultimately, McClintock's traveling street theatre took the form of a mobile community center, resounding with the studio's goals of healing, self-determination, and connection with diverse communities. Through this actor-centered street theatre, which broke traditional theatrical conventions, the actors presented facets of being Black in America. *Where It's At* featured the ensemble's common goal of protesting the hegemony, yet it also acknowledged the nuances of an actor's individual experience. By giving equal weight to the collective and the individual, *Where It's At* disrupted the notion of a monolithic Black experience yet acknowledged overlaps in experience while still calling for social justice and equality.

The Rose That Grew from Concrete

Tupac Shakur's oeuvre speaks to the artistic process of *Where It's At* in that his music and lyrics echoed his personal sociopolitical concerns, which resonated with Black communities across the country. The tenets of self-determination and community building, two priorities in McClintock's technique and aesthetic, reverberate in Tupac's music. McClintock's mentorship of a preteen Tupac certainly demonstrates McClintock's profound influence on one of the most prolific hip-hop artists of the twenty-first century. Yet many narratives about Tupac do not include his early education in Jazz Acting, which took place long before the artist's rise to stardom.

In McClintock's production of *The Rose That Grew from Concrete*, created a decade before the Broadway musical *Holla If Ya Hear Me*, the ensemble celebrated Tupac's legacy, vision, and artistic mastery of language, countering narratives of the stereotypical thug. Though Tupac Shakur exuded heteronormative masculinity, he had a close relationship with Ernie McClintock from the time Tupac first walked into the 127th Street Repertory Ensemble until his untimely death in 1996. *The Rose that Grew from Concrete*, McClintock's homage to Tupac Shakur, demonstrates the synergy and spiritual connection between the two. In September 1983, Tupac's mother, Afeni Shakur, a former Black Panther and activist, enrolled Tupac in the 127th Street Repertory Ensemble. In 2015, hip-hop scholar James Spady published an article based on an interview conducted with Tupac at least twenty years prior: "In addition to being a gifted and learned poet/philosopher, Tupac was a superb dramatist with over five years of formal training."[14] Twelve-year-old Tupac was cast as the understudy for Travis Younger in Lorraine Hansberry's *A Raisin in the Sun*, where he learned by both watching the elders of the company and performing onstage.

McClintock's 1984 production of *A Raisin in the Sun* at the Apollo Theater was part of a fundraising effort for Jesse Jackson's presidential campaign.

Longtime friend and studio member Hazel Rosetta Smith recalled how Tupac mouthed the words of the play as the actors rehearsed.[15] She was unsure whether he was imitating, marking, or memorizing. When the young actor who was initially cast as Travis left the show midway through the process, Tupac stepped in and knew every word written by Hansberry. According to his ensemble members—including Levy Lee Simon, who played Walter Lee, and Hazel Rosetta Smith, a swing—the young Tupac was magnetic onstage and viscerally connected to language, foreshadowing his own career and fame as a poet and hip-hop artist.[16] In reflecting on his own performance, a twentysomething Tupac was humbled: "I didn't know what I was doing back then even though I was good at everything, I wish I had them [Hazel Smith and Ernie McClintock] now because they were both great actors."[17]

As with all his students, the connection between McClintock and Tupac extended beyond performing in a play or practicing acting techniques. Significantly, students also admired and loved Ronald Walker, McClintock's life partner of more than thirty years. Walker was an innovative set and lighting designer who also functioned as the technical director. An image of Tupac, Ronald Walker, and McClintock standing in front of a poster for El Hajj Malik is a powerful visual representation of McClintock's legacy (figure 3.2). At the height of Tupac's fame, he returned to Richmond to visit his early mentor, who was philosophically aligned with Black Power. Many of Tupac's lyrics focused on healing the community, self-determination, and connecting generations. For example, his 1993 song "Keep Ya Head Up" was dedicated

Figure 3.2. Ronald Walker, Tupac Shakur, and Ernie McClintock in front of a poster for the Jazz Actors Theatre's production of N. R. Davidson's El Hajj Malik. Courtesy of the Private Collection of Geno Brantley.

to his godson Elijah and "a little girl Corinne," the future generations in the African American continuum in which he asserts the importance of women and questions why women are so mistreated. The song's lyrics express how society is overdue in lifting up Black women and calls for the collective to take an active role in healing past traumas, including sexual assault. McClintock's training of Black actors helped them develop the skills to self-define through healing, with the intention of then healing their communities.

Echoing the structure of *Where It's At*, *The Rose that Grew from Concrete* is not a traditional scripted play with distinct characters, plot, rising action, climax, and falling action, as the Aristotelian structure dictates. The theatrical piece "combined a mix of modern and African dance and poetry, hip-hop themed soliloquies and some R&B musical selections."[18] McClintock created the play, which was part of the annual Black Theatre Festival in Richmond, to highlight how hip-hop and Tupac's contribution to music and art could reach multiple generations and audiences.

The play was performed in early August 2002, at the Firehouse Theatre on West Broad Street, to a full audience. The cast included six women from Richmond's City Dance Troupe, five male actors, and a two-man percussion and guitar ensemble. Reviewer Holly M. Rodriguez reported that "the production created an experience that carried the audience through a roller coaster of emotions from happiness and excitement to fear and loneliness, and in the end, peace."[19] The peace was reflected in a final dance routine by five couples, choreographed by Rodney Williams, that wavered between modern dance and ballet. The notion of peace is important because hip-hop can often reflect a community's outrage, yet there are also ways to leverage that outrage to demand a more productive and equitable society. In an interview, Williams told Rodriguez that "producing black theater in Richmond is a struggle, but there is strong potential for growth here. 'It's always hard—the arts have to struggle for a voice,' he said. 'But I thank God for people like Ernie McClintock, because it takes someone like him, someone with persistence and dedication to the craft, to make it work.'"[20] McClintock undoubtedly passed along his work ethic and "dedication to the craft" to Tupac, echoing Ron Karenga's 1968 assertion that Black art should be "revolutionary. In brief, functional, collective, and committing."[21] *The Rose That Grew from Concrete* accomplished these goals by featuring the poetry, power, and activism of Tupac Shakur through an aesthetic rooted in the collective culture within the diaspora.

Ndangered

One of McClintock's last productions in the festival, *Ndangered*, exemplified the actor-centered Jazz Acting approach to collectively authored pieces. *Ndangered* highlighted critical issues that continue to face young Black men, including incarceration, the absence of a father in family life, peer pressure, sexually transmitted infections, and racism. Much like *Rose*, the production countered narratives of a one-dimensional thug stereotype, yet differed in that these men were from the Richmond community and brought their nuanced perspectives to content creation. This particular production, modeled after *Where It's At* in terms of approach and process, was first performed before an audience in 1999. McClintock and his actors then continued to evolve the piece for the next four years. Similar to *Rose*, *Ndangered* is not a play per se but a theatrical piece that foregrounds the concerns of young Black men. It was a way to give artistic agency to actors and provide space for them to share their individualized and collective experiences with audiences. Its premise that young Black men are an endangered species forces audiences to confront stereotypes of Black men as subhuman while highlighting their ontological experiences in Richmond (figure 3.3).

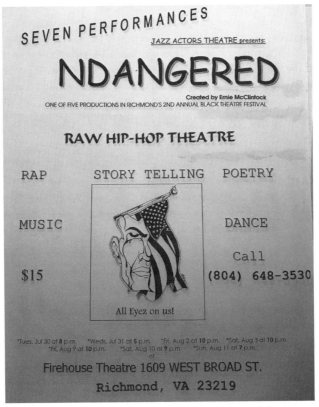

Figure 3.3. Advertisement for Ndangered. Courtesy of the Private Collection of Geno Brantley.

In 1999, *Ndangered* toured Richmond, New York, and Winston-Salem, North Carolina. It received mixed reviews. Michael J. Venable described the opening moments of the piece: "The auditorium was dimly lit and spooky; a nervous audience sat hushed. The ringleader appeared first, cracking his whip while his booming voice introduced the circus. Crew members then wheeled out animals under the red light—endangered black creatures clad in loin cloths, howling, screeching and pawing through the bars that confined them. . . . Concocting amazing speech patterns, they angrily lashed out at demons inhabiting hip-hop culture."[22] The 1999 cast included Haige Brown, Charles Green, Brother Juarez, Iman Shabazz, Kenya Gadson, Naadir Studevent, and Jeffrey Page, who choreographed the piece. In an influential 1999 article in *American Theatre* about hip-hop theatre, Holly Bass acknowledged the striking images but wrote that the show "fails to draw a clear connection between the many forms of black arts represented in the vignettes and their contribution to hip-hop."[23] Although this critique may be valid, Bass did not indicate what those connections should have been or why it is necessary for a theatrical piece to specify a contribution to hip-hop. I assert that the point of McClintock's piece was to stage an authentic theatrical work of young actors responding to their immediate environment—a common theme in hip-hop and therefore a direct contribution to the genre. Although Bass critiqued *Ndangered*, she nonetheless established him and his theatre company as part of the initial phase of hip-hop theatre's development.

McClintock asked each actor to "bring something real and significant to this piece that helps tell the contemporary story of young black men in America,"[24] including free verse, songs, dramatizations, comic moments, and audience participation. Venable asserted, "*Ndangered* combined emotions and thoughts that all young black men have once confronted in some capacity. It is fresh, fast-paced, dynamic, daring, and very, very real."[25] The vulnerability required of these young actors, steered by McClintock, to create such a piece demonstrates the notion of his studio as a "temple of healing."[26] Performers engaging with painful subject matter could feel triggered and potentially relive past traumas. However, through Jazz Acting and McClintock's approach to the rehearsal process, *Ndangered* was a theatrical site of truth and a sacred experience.

When *Ndangered* was presented at the tenth National Black Theatre Festival in Winston-Salem, reviewer Linda Armstrong applauded the production's content and form, in particular how it "looked at the young Black man's desperate need to be encouraged and loved by Black women and it touched on how Black men must take care of each other."[27] She further highlighted the smooth and well-thought-out production value, with an emphasis on "a young man's spiritual development."[28] The degree of vulnerability in the *Ndangered* series came as a result of McClintock demanding a high standard of excellence and challenging his actors to create and perform beyond their comfort zones. Notably, McClintock's observation that audiences were surprised by the caliber of the performance demonstrates that even in the last few years of his life, preconceived notions about him persisted, perhaps due to his vanguard queer positionality. Specifically, an out gay man facilitating the creative process of a hip-hop production with topics that are usually associated with Black masculinity ruptured the notion that queerness and hip-hop are antithetical.

Conclusion

By tracing McClintock's collectively authored pieces from their beginnings as street theatre in the 1960s to their development into hip-hop theatre in the 1990s, McClintock emerges as an early facilitator of hip-hop theatre. In *Where It's At*, *The Rose That Grew from Concrete*, and *Ndangered*, the director was consistently concerned with his students identifying their sociopolitical concerns and connecting to the community, which for many actors engendered self-discovery. Jazz Actor, activist, and *Ndangered* performer Iman Shabazz observed, "The [training] was beyond just helping me become a better actor. It was helping me to become a better man who understood our culture and the connections of that culture to the work we were doing and then how it impacted the rest of the community."[29] Shabazz's words hearken to the foundational principles that remained consistent throughout McClintock's career: self-expression as self-determination and ensemble as community. This construct of self-expression and community building offered a multiplicity of Black perspectives while unifying respective communities to subvert the hegemony.

Notes

1. Doris Freedman, "Ernie McClintock," New York Public Radio, August 30, 1970.
2. Author interview with Marc Primus, Atlanta, George, August 25, 2015.
3. Daniel Banks, "Introduction: Hip Hop Theater's Ethic of Inclusion," in *Say Word! Voices from Hip Hop Theater*, ed. Daniel Banks (Ann Arbor: University of Michigan Press, 2011), 1–23.
4. Banks, "Introduction," 1.
5. Nicole Hodges Persley, "Hip-hop Theater and Performance," in *The Cambridge Companion to Hip-Hop*, ed. Justin A. Williams (Cambridge: Cambridge University Press, 2015), 87.
6. Banks, "Introduction," 17–18.
7. Hodges Persley, "Hip-hop Theater and Performance," 85–98.

8. Paul Carter Harrison, "Praise/Word," in *Black Theatre: Ritual Performance in the African Diaspora*, ed. Paul Carter Harrison, Victor Leo Walker II, and Gus Edwards (Philadelphia, PA: Temple University Press, 2002), 1–12.

9. "Black Theatre Companies: Afro-American Theatre (Ernie McClintock), 1970–1983," Errol G. Hill Papers, Rauner Special Collections Library, Dartmouth College.

10. Harrison, "Praise/Word," 7.

11. William Chafe, *The Unfinished Journey*, 3rd ed., ed. Nancy Lane (New York: Oxford University Press, 1995), 391.

12. Mance Williams, *Black Theatre in the 1960s and 1970s: A Historical-Critical Analysis of the Movement* (Westport, CT: Greenwood, 1985), 47.

13. McClandish Phillips, "1250 Performances Are Given Here during Season," *New York Times*, August 27, 1970, 41.

14. James Spady, "Tupac Amaru Shakur: Lights Dimmed, Drama, Epistemologies, Cultural Transformations and the Rights/Rites of Memory," *ScoopUSA*, July 17, 2015, 7. Spady's article does not include the date of his interview with the hip-hop artist. Spady was a leading scholar in hip-hop studies. For more in-depth information, refer to his books *Nation Conscious Rap* (Brooklyn, NY: PC International, 1991), *Twisted Tales: In the Hip Hop Streets of Philly* (Philadelphia: UMUM/LOH Publishers,1995), and *Street Conscious Rap* (Philadelphia: UMUM/LOH Publishers, 1999). These works include interviews with more than sixty artists, including Tupac Shakur.

15. Author's interview with Hazel Smith via Zoom, August 11, 2021.

16. In the 127th Street Repertory Company, even if an actor was not cast in a production, they would be integrated into the process. This could be as an understudy, as part of backstage crew, in costumes, or wherever the show needed support. Therefore, they would still be integral to the production and learn by doing as well as by watching McClintock's rehearsal process.

17. Spady, "Tupac Amaru Shakur," 7.

18. Holly Rodriguez, "Listening to Black Voices," *Style Weekly* (website), August 14, 2002.

19. Rodriguez, "Listening to Black Voices."

20. Rodriguez, "Listening to Black Voices."

21. Ron Karenga, "Black Nationalism," in *The Black Aesthetic*, ed. Gayle Addison Jr. (Garden City, NY: Doubleday, 1971), 32–38.

22. Michael J. Venable, "Ndangered Acts in Mysterious Ways," *Richmond Times-Dispatch*, August 10, 1999, D3.

23. Holly Bass, "Blowin' Up the Set," *American Theatre* 16, no. 9 (1999): 18–20.

24. Venable, "Ndangered Acts in Mysterious Ways," D3.

25. Venable, "Ndangered Acts in Mysterious Ways," D3.

26. Primus, interview.

27. Linda Armstrong, "10th Anniversary of Black Theater Fest Boasts Pride," *New York Amsterdam News*, August 12, 1999, 27:1.

28. Armstrong, "10th Anniversary of Black Theater Fest Boasts Pride," 1.

29. Author's interview with Iman Shabazz, Richmond, Virginia, September 9, 2015.

Performing Pilgrimage

Popular Religious Education at Chautauqua's Palestine Park

Chelsea Taylor

"PALESTINE IS BURIED, mountains, seas, walks, and even the Lake, with a great thickness of ice and snow on it, stretching down in front of the Holy Land for miles, presents a snowy, freezing coldness."[1] To the unfamiliar reader, the *Chautauqua Assembly Daily Herald*'s opening of the 1877 spring supplement to the newspaper may seem ominous if not outright apocalyptic. After all, how could Jerusalem with its characteristically warm and arid Mediterranean climate be covered in such a layer of snow and ice? And yet, nineteenth-century readers of the *Herald* would find this weather report to be completely expected, since "Palestine" here refers to the Chautauqua Assembly's replica of the Holy Land in western New York called Palestine Park or, occasionally, the Park of Palestine.

In 1874, Reverend John Heyl Vincent and Lewis Miller founded the Chautauqua Assembly (now known as the Chautauqua Institution) as an ecumenical spiritual and educational retreat for Christians on Chautauqua Lake in western New York. Within its first decade, the Chautauqua Assembly grew into a thriving center that combined religious popular education with middle-class summer vacationing, offering guests a variety of programming including lectures, costumed performances, leisure activities, and Bible study courses. As Charlotte M. Canning argues in her book *The Most American Thing in America*, Chautauqua's immense popularity led to its further commercialization to the point that more than nine thousand circuit "Chautauquas" had been developed and had toured nationally by 1921.[2] One of Chautauqua's earliest and most popular attractions was Palestine Park, an outdoor, scaled replica of the Holy Land that provided a walkable relief map for the study of biblical geography. "That wonder of wonders," as the *Herald* describes it, is "the very best representation of the ancient Lord's Land in America" where "thousands upon thousands" have studied the geography of scripture.[3]

While the *Herald* and other promotional materials consistently acclaim the accuracy, authenticity, and pedagogical value of Palestine Park, guest experiences at times describe the park as uninspiring or even unrecognizable as the Holy Land in the absence of performance. So much so that when famous English writer Rudyard Kipling visited the park in the late 1880s, he described the area simply as an "artificial hillocks surrounding a mud puddle and a wormy streak of slime connecting it to another mud puddle."[4] Despite Chautauqua's framing of the park as "a work of art truer to nature," Kipling was not the only guest who found Palestine Park underwhelming or even illegible when encountering it on their own. On July 31, 1889, the Herald announced that "the little raised iron plates" displaying maps of biblical cities "dotted here and there over the Model of Palestine are not mud scrapers, as some of our visitors evidently think."[5] This comical misuse of the plaques (which were only slightly raised above the ground) further shows how visitors could walk through the park without recognizing its referent at all. And yet, the *Herald* continually lauded the park as "accurate and invaluable" to the mission of Chautauqua, going as far as to claim, "Palestine Park has but one equal, and that is Palestine itself."[6]

Why, then, did this potentially underwhelming space become an "immediate success" among guests at the end of the long nineteenth century?[7] I assert that the Park of Palestine's popularity during the late-nineteenth and early-twentieth centuries was inherently tied to performances within the park, undertaken by both professional performers and guests, that enabled visitors to experience surrogate pilgrimages and imagine what it would be like to walk where Jesus walked. By analyzing Chautauqua's newspaper and magazine publications alongside fictional novels about vacationing at Chautauqua, I reveal how the assembly encouraged guests to engage with their constructed replica by inviting them to perform as biblical people during scheduled events in the park, such as costumed lectures and geography classes. By repeatedly framing these performances as acts of pilgrimage, Chautauqua's founders inspired guests to understand and interact with a potentially underwhelming physical space in western New York as if it was the sacred land of Jesus's birth, death, and resurrection. Although Palestine Park's popularity dramatically decreased after the 1920s, this nineteenth-century experimentation with vacation learning developed forms of performance-based, interactive pedagogy so popular that their traces can still be seen at religious edutainment centers in the United States today.[8]

The Catholic tradition of physically embarking on surrogate pilgrimages using devotional practices such as walking prayer labyrinths or following the Stations of the Cross (*via Crucis*) has a long history reaching back to Europe's Middle Ages.[9] However, this new opportunity for surrogate pilgrimage would have most likely been a novel experience for Chautauqua's predominantly Protestant patrons, whose religious denominations developed out of the Protestant Reformation's rejection of Catholicism's material culture. I posit that Chautauqua's Palestine Park serves as an early example of a specifically American Protestant tradition of surrogate pilgrimage rooted in pedagogy of biblical geography and Orientalism. While Catholic devotional traditions of surrogate pilgrimage provided and embodied experience that encouraged spiritual reflection and contemplation, they lacked the connection to the Holy Land itself, with all its perceived exotic novelty, that nineteenth-century American Protestants yearned for due to the development of a new middle-class tourism industry. As Burke O. Long writes in *Imagining the Holy Land*, "infatuation with the Holy Land had shifted from conceiving it as a non-earthly utopian space—imagined in poetry, song, and liturgy—to an idealized, touchable place—a fantasized reality on the ground."[10] A trend of teaching biblical geography through lectures with visual aids, published guidebooks, and miniature models emerged to meet the demands of this Holy Land infatuation. However, these forms of popular education failed to provide that embodied devotional experience that aspiring pilgrims craved. Through Palestine Park, the Chautauqua Assembly combined the bodily experience of pilgrimage with popular education and, in doing so, made real a "fantasized reality on the ground."[11]

"The Ancient Lord's Land in America": Building an American Holy Land

The earliest iteration of Palestine Park, preserved in a photograph taken by George G. Johnston in 1874 titled "Valley of the Jordan from the Summit of Mount Hermon," consisted of a rocky landscape with a small, dumbbell-shaped ditch framed by slightly elevated hills and pathways.[12] The area, a quarter of the size of an American football field, appears as if could have formed naturally by rainwater collecting in the muddy crevices between rocks and grass-covered knolls. If the title and accompanying inscription featured on the back of the image had not specifically labeled Holy Land landmarks like Mount Hermon, the Dead Sea, and the Sea of Galilee, viewers of the image could easily mistake the carefully designed park for a quaint, albeit rugged lakeside walking trail.

Palestine Park was originally built as a scaled relief map by Rev. W. W. Wythe at the bequest of Vincent "to provide a large map or model of the Holy Land for the instruction of teachers and young people who are interested in Bible History."[13] Constructed with fallen tree trunks, sawdust, soil, grass, and man-made ditches, the original design of the park aimed to replicate the topography of Palestine only temporarily, built just to survive the peak summer season. Occupying a 120-by-75-foot area, the walkable map used a scale of twenty-one inches to one mile to represent width and length and an exaggerated scale of thirteen feet to one mile for height. This small area provided guests with an aerial view, or a God-like perspective, of the Holy Land, allowing lecturers to trace the travel routes of biblical figures. Although Chautauqua's construction team kept strictly to these scales as a means of maintaining accuracy and claiming authenticity, they also made the peculiar choice of reversing the cardinal directions of the park, making north represent south and east represent west. Ultimately, the natural positioning of Chautauqua Lake (a large body of water ideal for representing the Mediterranean Sea) dictated this choice, seeing as Chautauqua Lake sits east of the Palestine Park while the Mediterranean Sea sits west of the Holy Land. In *The Story of Chautauqua*, Jesse L. Hurlburt excuses this odd orientation by writing: "But the sun persists in its independence, rises over Chautauqua's Mediterranean Sea where it should set, and continues its sunset over the mountains of Gilead, where it should rise. Dr. Vincent and Lewis Miller could bring to pass some remarkable, even seemingly impossible, achievements, but they were not able to outdo Joshua, and not only make the sun stand still, but set it moving in a direction opposite to its natural course."[14] Despite this potentially confusing reversal, the site transformed from a simple pedagogical tool into a popular tourist attraction, due to its novelty and an increased amount of scheduled programming in the park. By the summer of 1880, the park's reputation had spread to the point that then presidential candidate General James A. Garfield reported he had heard of Palestine Park and specifically asked Vincent for a tour, drawing a remarkable crowd to the area.[15]

The park underwent several reconstructions in an effort to keep it "worthy of Chautauqua."[16] In 1879, Rev. Dr. William Henry Perrine, a minister and professor known for his expertise in Holy Land studies, refashioned the park with more durable materials, like concrete and cast metal, and expanded it to a total of 350 square feet. Similarly, in 1907, Rev. Alfred D. Barrows refurbished the landscape and authored a guidebook for visitors, which was later revised by Hurlbut and republished in 1920. While Palestine Park remains intact as a walkable space on the Chautauqua Institution's campus to this day, the park lost its prominence as a major attraction among Chautauqua's programming after the 1920s. David Taylor's 1936 *Guide Book to Palestine Park* acknowledges the decreased amount of events, classes, and activity in the park and introduces the preservation of the space as commemorative act honoring "the men whose early vision produced it."[17] This subtle shift in Chautauqua's framing of the park marks its diminished popularity and ostensibly decommissions the site after sixty years of guest engagement.

Palestine Park's rise and fall in popularity reflects a larger, national trend of America's fascination with the Holy Land over the course of the long nineteenth century. Scholars such as Stephanie Stidham Rogers, John Davis, Burke O. Long, Brian Yothers, Lester Irwin Vogel, and Lenny Ben-David examine America's fascination with Palestine in the nineteenth century by documenting the pilgrimages, tours, and research expeditions taken by American Protestants and tracing the circulation of the materials they brought back, such as photographs, relics, souvenirs, and travelogues.[18] These written travel accounts and material objects paved the way for religious entrepreneurs to bring the Holy Land stateside through a variety of entertainment forms, including meticulously illustrated travel books, painted panoramic murals, traveling lectures with photographic visual aids, three-dimensional models of Jerusalem, cabinets of curiosities featuring Holy Land relics, and, eventually, full-scale replicas.

As Long illustrates, American replicas of the Holy Land embody a "curious mix of romantic imagination, historical rectitude, and attachment to a physical space" that satisfy this emerging nineteenth-century "thirst for the 'real' land of revelation."[19] For example, the 1904 St. Louis World's Fair, the Louisiana Purchase Exposition, presented a full-scale replica of Jerusalem by recreating three hundred structures and twenty-two streets in its ten-acre Jerusalem Exhibit. Similarly, Gerald L.K. Smith built the "New Holy Land"—a two-hour interactive tour featuring a full-scale Wilderness Tabernacle replica, a pond representing the Sea of Galilee, and a re-creation of the Last Supper's Upper Room—as one of his many "Sacred Projects" in Eureka Springs, Arkansas. Long observes that Chautauqua's Palestine Park, no matter how underwhelming it may appear, serves as a crucial historical antecedent to these more spectacular American Holy Lands.[20]

Furthermore, a wealth of scholarship has developed over the last two decades examining how performances at twentieth- and twenty-first-century American Holy Lands impact popular culture and religiosity in the United States. Jill Stevenson, in her book *Sensational Devotion*, argues that such sites, like the Holy Land Experience in Orlando, Florida, cultivate religious belief by creating vivid, sensual devotional experiences for guests and shape national discourses on a wide range of political issues.[21] Similarly, in *Preaching to Convert*, John Fletcher reveals the evangelical tactics, or "outreach strategies," inherent to the dramaturgy of immersive places like creation museums, hell houses, and megachurches.[22] Exploring apocalyptic evangelical performances at Christian tourist destinations like Sight & Sound Theatres and the Holy Land Experience, Kristin Dombek shows how sectarian and secular cultures share an obsession with the end-times that contributes to a particular brand of consumerism.[23] I argue that the tourist destinations explored by these authors, and their subsequent spiritual, cultural, and political impacts, were possible because Chautauqua's Palestine Park paved the way for more elaborate forms of Protestant surrogate pilgrimage to develop.

Promoting Surrogate Pilgrimage: Modeling
Guest Engagement with Palestine Park

Vincent, before founding the Chautauqua Assembly, understood this craving or thirst for the land of revelation and believed that "intimate knowledge of the topography of Palestine was basic to Christian morals, if not salvation."[24] In 1863, Vincent took a pilgrimage to Palestine and Egypt and was deeply moved by the experience. In a biography based on Vincent's personal papers and journals, Leon Vincent recounts his uncle's experience: "But there can be no doubt as to the character of the impressions resulting from his stay in the Holy Land; they were deep and lasting. He was profoundly moved as he gazed on scenes that were to him of the highest significance in that they formed the background and setting of a great drama—a drama the essential truth of which, historical or religious, he never questioned."[25] While this journey reinforced Vincent's lifelong passion for teaching biblical geography, it was not without its difficulties and inconveniences. In his personal papers, he often complained about the "dirty" conditions of both the housing accommodations and the local people and reported being disturbed by "fleas that crawled all over us and dogs outside . . . barking all night."[26] Inspired by his own pilgrimage, Vincent aimed not just to replicate the Holy Land's topography at Chautauqua but also to communicate this powerful feeling of imagining the drama of the Bible unfolding before your very eyes. And yet, he wished to do so in a way that avoided all the inconveniences Americans may encounter when traveling abroad.

Chautauqua's early promotional materials framed visiting Palestine Park as an act of surrogate pilgrimage. Perhaps most American Christians could not afford the long, arduous journey through the Ottoman Empire, but they could manage a brief stay at a religious retreat in western New York and enjoy a similar, more convenient, experience. The *Herald*'s 1876 announcement of the reopening of the park illustrates this framework by guiding the reader on a fanciful journey, stating: "We present the salient features of the sacred land, where lived Jacob, Joseph, Samuel, Saul, David, Solomon, and above all and greater than all—the Lord Jesus, who lived and died and rose in Palestine, and from Palestine he ascended into Heaven. We are now prepared to make a pilgrimage through the Park of Palestine. Imagine yourself coming in from the south and traveling northward. Let us go at once to Jerusalem, the ancient capital of the country, and from that city take a survey of the land."[27] This article actively invites readers to "imagine" themselves traveling the landscape as pilgrims, emphasizing that they are figuratively following in the steps of biblical heroes. As a promotional article, it models how one should experience the park before the visitor actually interacts with the constructed, scaled replica. By narrating a future encounter, the author not only guides the reader's future interpretation of the site but also sets the stage for an imagined drama in which the reader takes on a biblical character similar to that of "Jacob, Joseph, Samuel, Saul, David, Solomon." The author gestures to the collapse of time in the park, making the land of the Bible ahistorical: visitors can imagine the Old and New Testaments simultaneously without abandoning their present reality.

Furthermore, the term "pilgrimage" is consistently used by Chautauqua's publications to describe even the most mundane events in the park. By doing so, these publications subtly urge guests to accept the park as a worthy substitute for the actual Holy Land, heightening the park's importance. For example, the *Herald* announced that rain prevented the children's class from going to Palestine, so "the pilgrimage will be taken some other time."[28] Similarly, the newspaper advertised "a course of study in the Boys' and Girls' Class in the geography of the Bible" during which "pilgrimages through the Park of Palestine will be made."[29] These constant references to pilgrimage continually ask visitors to treat a trip to the park like one to the sacred ground of the Bible while simultaneously recognizing their participation in a constructed, pedagogical experience on Chautauqua Lake.

In this light, Chautauqua's Palestine Park exemplifies the same intrinsic paradoxes of the theatre: The phenomenological acceptance of a constructed falsehood allows for a deeper belief in the semiotic or represented fantasy. Bert O. States's concept of binocular vision can be illustrated through the example of an audience member watching a talented actor.[30] As spectators come to believe the character is real, they simultaneously recognize the actor's virtuosity. Similarly, the more spectators engage with the promotional framework of pilgrimage, which frequently asks them to imagine themselves as biblical people in the Levant, the more they appreciate the novelty of Chautauqua's immersive pedagogy. Unlike its contemporaries, which evoked fantasies of the Holy Land through images and small material objects, Chautauqua rooted these fantasies in a physical space, ostensibly creating the opportunity for a bodily experience of pilgrimage in this American Holy Land.

On August 8, 1883, the *Herald* published yet another narrativized journey through the park in its article "The Point." Toward the conclusion, the article asks readers to "turn now to Palestine, that wonderful land by the Lake, where you can visit all the regions of the Holy Land without weariness or trouble."[31] Here, the newspaper artfully reinforces readers' binocular vision by promising them an experience of pilgrimage while acknowledging the convenience of having an American replica that relieves visitors from the "weariness" and "trouble" of visiting the actual Holy Land. Guests at Chautauqua could, perhaps, be spared from the nighttime fleas and barking dogs that Vincent suffered on his own pilgrimage. The article encourages readers to believe in the "realness" of the park's connection with biblical sites while appreciating all the intended benefits and comforts of summer resort life.

Chautauqua's encouragement of binocular vision can also be seen throughout the *Herald*'s serialized novel "Story of Miss Ida Norton at Chautauqua," by Reverend H. H. Moore. Chapter 10 of the story, printed on August 16, 1877, reads: "In the Park of Palestine, [Charles] was standing in a crowd of people who were listening to Mr. Van Lennep, who was explaining the topography and Bible History of the Holy Land. . . . While he spoke of Gethsemane it was noticed that Pauline gave close and tearful attention. She was heard to say to herself in a whisper, 'For me, for me—was shed for me.'"[32] While chapter 10 only briefly mentions the Park of Palestine, it demonstrates how impactful the park can be as an essential backdrop for both planned lectures and guest revelations. Rather than simply reporting on the lecture itself or retelling the narrative of Christ's Passion, "The Story of Miss Ida Norton at Chautauqua" strategically dramatizes the power of understanding both, highlighting Pauline's emotional reaffirmation of faith after learning about the geography of Gethsemane. Pauline's experience mirrors Vincent's account of his 1863 pilgrimage, which frames the Holy Land as an essential setting for the Bible's drama. In doing so, this fictionalized account of Chautauqua models surrogate pilgrimage within the park, advertising the potential for enlivened religious belief through popular education.

Chautauqua's promotional model of surrogate pilgrimage is slightly different from the long-standing Catholic versions, such as labyrinths and the Stations of the Cross. While Palestine Park follows the Catholic tradition of providing a built environment that facilitates "a tangible connection between persons across time, those who have come before and all those who will come again," it does so by replicating specific place-based pilgrimage rather than a devotional practice marking a spiritual journey.[33] Prayer labyrinths, like the one in Chartres Cathedral, encourage a form of walking meditation by providing a complex circular pathway that serves as a physical reminder of one's spiritual journey toward salvation through Christ.[34] Similarly, following the Stations of the Cross is a devotional practice usually performed in the season of Lent, during which members of the church travel between markers within or outside of the church that visually represent key scenes from Christ's passion. These markers can take a variety of forms, from stained glass windows and simple plaques to elaborate *tableaux vivants* created by costumed performers. The Stations of the Cross more closely resemble place-based pilgrimage, because the practice replicates traveling the Via Dolorosa (Way of Suffering), which traces Jesus's path through the Old City of Jerusalem to Mount Calvary. However, the aim of each station is to inspire spiritual reflection by illustrating Christ's suffering for the sake of humanity, not to replicate specific sites in Jerusalem or to fulfill what Long describes as a nineteenth-century "thirst for the 'real' land of revelation."[35]

As an early, walkable Holy Land replica in the United States, Palestine Park established a new tradition of American Protestant surrogate pilgrimage rooted in forms of popular education. As James S. Bielo argues in *Materializing the Bible*, "since the mid-nineteenth century, Protestants have invested in technologies, techniques, programs, and institutions that rest on participatory pedagogy," and, as seen in Chautauqua's founding mission, Palestine Park is no exception.[36] After all, Vincent maintained that knowledge of biblical geography provided "strong and irresistible evidence in favor of [the Bible's] divinity" and that without it, "understand[ing] the divine word" would be "impossible."[37] Considering this extraordinary emphasis on pedagogy as a prerequisite for appreciating the foundational scripture of Christianity, it is no wonder the park seemed lackluster in the absence of performances. Without the promotional framework of pilgrimage or, as we will see in the next section, an experienced orator guiding the surrogate pilgrimages, the park lost its power to create that emotional connection to the Bible's "great drama" that Vincent experienced on his own pilgrimage. Simply put, without performance, Palestine Park was demoted from an essential backdrop for "The Greatest Story Ever Told" to an underwhelming lakeside trail.

Performing Pilgrimage: Costumed Lectures and Orientalism in Palestine Park

Within the first two seasons of Palestine Park's construction, the guests of Chautauqua went from simply imagining the drama of the Bible to re-enacting it through staged skits, costumed lectures, and participatory guest performances. Instead of simply appreciating the somewhat detached aerial view of the original walkable relief map, they saw the park's expanded mise-en-scène as an invitation to populate the replica with biblical characters of their own creation. Rather than engage with one of the more predominant forms of community-based, Christian Theatre, such as passion plays, cycle dramas, or morality plays, the Chautauqua Assembly quenched their "thirst" for the real Holy Land by performing as "Orientals," essentially fetishizing the racial and religious other who inhabited Ottoman Palestine at the turn of the twentieth century.[38] As Edward W. Said theorizes, "the Orient was almost a European invention, and had been since antiquity a place of romance, exotic beings, haunted memories and landscapes, remarkable experiences."[39] Similar, Chautauquans used Palestine Park to invent a romanticized view of what pilgrimage to Holy Land could be, combining a fantasized biblical past with an exotic yet sanitized present to specifically cater to late-nineteenth-century American sensibilities.

Reverend J. S. Ostrander was one of the earliest biblical geography lecturers to tap into this emerging culture of Orientalism at the resort. An 1876 photograph titled "Oriental Group on Palestine Park" shows him with about twenty guests standing on a grassy hill, ready to embark on their surrogate pilgrimage wearing a disparate collection of tunics, robes, cloaks, scarves, vests, turbans, and headscarves.[40] This photograph, documenting the eclectic European fantasy surrounding Middle Eastern wear, evidences the park as a site of play, where dressing in costume and taking on characters was deemed appropriate. Similarly, in August 1880, the *Herald* reports that Ostrander, "dressed in the costume of an ancient Asiatic [sic]," presented several "Oriental customs and manners," such as "weddings, funerals, and other scenes." Throughout the lecture, he was joined by participating audience members, like several women "dressed in Oriental style" who demonstrated the "Oriental method of carrying water" or a man modeling "the costume of a high priest" while Ostrander explained "the significance of his garments." Although the report briefly admonishes some of the performances, like the "Mohammedan prayer meeting," as "uncouth," it ultimately concludes: "Familiarity with these customs, costumes, rites, ceremonies, and law greatly aide us in understanding the Hebrew Scriptures."[41] Chautauquans' recognition of other Abrahamic religions and their attachment to the Holy Land was limited in that it existed only to deepen Christian understanding of the Bible, not to encourage a sense of religious pluralism. The costumes in these scenes mark guest desires to become the biblical people that inhabit the Holy Land of the Bible. Visiting Ottoman Palestine in their own clothes as Americans abroad seems, then, to fall short of the performance-enabled fantasy that Palestine Park offers. A pilgrimage to Palestine could only transport you across the globe, but a surrogate pilgrimage at Chautauqua promised the opportunity of traveling back in time to experience the "real" land of the Bible. Unlike Palestine's actual bloody history, this fantasy of the Holy Land and its "oriental" characters existed outside of violent conflicts and occupations that made pilgrimage a risky gambit for American Christians.

Another Chautauqua performer, August O. Van Lennep, a convert to Christianity from Islam and a pioneer salesman of Holy Land stereographs, not only frequently performed in the park as an "Oriental" character with native knowledge of biblical lands but also served as the curator of Chautauqua's cabinet of curiosities, the "Oriental House." Van Lennep, born in Smyrna (an ancient city on the Aegean coast of Anatolia) during the Ottoman period to his Hollander father and Turkish mother, leaned into his multicultural identity and dark-skinned appearance to foster a mystique of exoticism around his performances. For example, he was known to give brief speeches and answer guest questions in Turkish, he constantly carried a shepherd's staff and wore a turban, and he climbed to the roof of the Oriental House daily to issue a "strange imitation of the Mohammedan's calls to prayer" in Arabic.[42] Much like Ostrander's costumed interactive lectures, Van Lennep's performances provided a taste of exoticism rooted in western fantasies of the "Far East" while remaining within the bounds of Christian propriety. In contrast to other white and white-presenting Chautauquans, Van Lennep's authority was rooted in his lived experience and developed character, not in an academic or theological expertise like his Methodist coworkers. While his positionality at Chautauqua allowed him to become the de facto expert in Egyptology and gave him dominion over the Oriental House, it also came with a unique set of considerable drawbacks. In his book *The Chautauqua Moment*, Andrew C. Rieser highlights visitors' accounts that objectify Van Lennep as if he was also a biblical artifact on display.[43] Moreover, Hurlburt recounts how some guests "actually mocked the make-believe muezzin before his face."[44] However, several months after Van Lennep's death in 1883, the *Herald* published Hurlburt's heartfelt eulogy, which celebrated the popular performer as "a refined Chautauqua gentleman" and "true Christian, of deep and sincere experience, living in fellowship with his Lord."[45] By memorializing Van Lennep as a "true Christian," Hurlburt assures his fellow Chautauquans that the performer only play-acted as a Muslim, reaffirming Chautauqua as a solely Christian space.

Through his performances, Van Lennep mastered the ability to shift between both racial and religious identities to serve the somewhat contradictory goals of displaying the Christian piety that was central to Chautauqua's founding mission and authenticating guest experiences of surrogate pilgrimage. Van Lennep, with shepherd's staff in hand, often began tours of Palestine Park with "authentic" performances of Muslim religious practices but ended with a message of salvation through Christ. As Long observes, Van Lennep transformed "his vaguely Semitic, Jew/Muslim/biblical persona into the archetypal shepherd Jesus . . . to nudge his audience, those specially chosen, toward renewed Christian devotion."[46] By taking on the roles of cultural expert in the "Orient" and Christian preacher simultaneously, he embodied the goal of surrogate pilgrimage by providing that "tangible connection" across both time and space.

Through the costumed lectures and demonstrations of both Ostrander and Van Lennep, participating guests of the park effectively performed as biblical people, populating a romanticized, ahistorical Holy Land of their own creation. While some Chautauquans rejected these performances as "uncouth" or empty entertainments, they remained immensely popular for the first several decades of Chautauqua's existence. Once the performers were gone and Chautauqua stopped programming the biblical geography lectures that originally inspired the park's creation, attractions like Palestine Park and the Oriental House became spiritless and pedestrian, if not illegible as Holy Land replicas.

Conclusion

Palestine Park remains intact yet slightly cut off from the Chautauqua Institution's contemporary campus. Palestine Avenue, which once led to a variety of attractions including the "Great Pyramid" and the "Oriental House," no longer sees major foot traffic. Similarly, guests stopped traveling across the lake on steamships and no longer disembark on the shores of Palestine Park. Although it now rarely utilizes the park as an essential backdrop for biblical geography lectures, the Chautauqua Institution still offers guests a large variety of ecumenical educational programming. In a tragic turn of events, Chautauqua's educational programming made national headlines recently when an assassination attempt of Salman Rushdie took place during a literary festival event on August 12, 2022. While reporting on the violent attack, NPR correspondent Jim Zarroli described Chautauqua as a "friendly, earnest place for serious conversation and quiet contemplation, where crime is practically nonexistent and the realities of the outside world can seem a long way off."[47] In this light, while a lot has changed at Chautauqua in the past century, its core mission of providing a tranquil religious retreat remains steadfast, even in the face of shocking violence on its campus.

Ultimately, Palestine Park's popularity ended with a whimper, not a bang. However, that should not take away from the historical significance of this nineteenth-century phenomenon. For several decades, performances not only created a new iteration of surrogate pilgrimage but also had the power to briefly sanctify the park as sacred ground in its own right. In *Old Chautauqua Days*, Theodore L. Flood describes the simplicity and immense value of Palestine Park, saying one needs only a talented guide to understand that this place was "made sacred by eloquence and song and lofty purpose inspired in human souls."[48] Furthermore, Hurlburt recounts how students in Palestine Park would "even pluck and preserve a spear of grass, carefully enshrining it in an envelope duly marked," because they thought "that soil from the Holy Land itself had been spread upon the park, constituting it a sort of Campo Santo."[49] By exploring how an underwhelming "mud-puddle," as Kipling would have it, could inspire a trend of surrogate pilgrimage among nineteenth-century Protestant Americans, we actually uncover the powerful, albeit ephemeral, influence of performance on acts of religious devotion.

Palestine Park remains a crucial precursor to the spectacle-heavy, religious edutainment centers that American Christians visit today. The impulse to invent and reinvent distinctly American versions of the Holy Land still thrives at sites like The Great Passion Play in Eureka Springs, Arkansas; The Shrine of Christ's Passion in St. John, Indiana; The Museum of the Bible in Washington, DC; and many, many more.[50] Furthermore, the promotional materials of these sites still advertise surrogate pilgrimage rooted in interactive pedagogy, making claims like "You don't have to go to the Holy Land!" and "Experience the world's greatest journey, now in VR!"[51] Although these contemporary spaces, virtual or physical, may look radically different, they still depend on the similar tactics used by Palestine Park, most notably incorporating performance to enable surrogate pilgrimage.

Notes

1. "Fair Point in the Winter," *Chautauqua Assembly Daily Herald*, Supplement 1 (May 10, 1877): 1.

2. Charlotte M. Canning, *The Most American Thing in America: Circuit Chautauqua as Performance* (Iowa City: University of Iowa Press, 2005).

3. "Fair Point in the Winter," *Chautauqua Assembly Daily Herald*, 1.

4. Burke O. Long, *Imagining the Holy Land* (Bloomington: Indiana University Press, 2003), 39.

5. "Drift of the Day," *Chautauqua Assembly Herald* 14, no. 7 (July 31, 1889): 1.

6. "Fair Point," *Chautauqua Assembly Daily Herald* 1, no. 1 (June 15, 1876): 2; "Models at Chautauqua," *Chautauqua Assembly Herald* 12, Advancement 2 (June 1887): 7.

7. John Davis, *The Landscape of Belief: Encountering the Holy Land in Nineteenth-Century American Art and Culture* (Princeton, NJ: Princeton University Press, 1996), 89.

8. James S. Bielo, *Materializing the Bible: Scripture, Sensation, Place* (London: Bloomsbury Academic, 2021). As Bielo observes, contemporary American Holy Land replicas take on a variety of forms including biblical gardens, theme parks, museums, and roadside attractions. The most popular sites usually combine several forms, offering their guests a wide variety of attractions. For example, The Holy Land Experience, a theme park that operated from 2001 to 2020 in Orlando, Florida, offered guests re-creations of both the Garden of Eden and the Garden of Gethsemane, an immersive Bible museum, and several musical shows retelling stories from the Bible. Similar examples currently in operation include: Answers in Genesis's Creation Museum and Ark Encounter; the Green Family's Museum of the Bible; and the "Sacred Projects" of The Great Passion Play organization.

9. Kathryn Barush, "The Root of the Route: Phil's Camino Project and the Catholic Tradition of Surrogate Pilgrimage," *Practical Matters Journal* 9 (2016): 70–80.

10. Long, *Imagining the Holy Land*, 2.

11. Long, *Imagining the Holy Land*, 2.

12. "Valley of the Jordan from the Summit of Mount Hermon," c. 1874, Stereo View on 7"×4" card frame, Chautauqua Institution Archives.

13. "Fair Point," *Chautauqua Assembly Daily Herald*, 2.

14. Jesse Lyman Hurlburt, *The Story of Chautauqua* (New York: G.P. Putnam's Sons, 1921), 48.

15. Hurlburt, *The Story of Chautauqua*, 182–83.

16. Hurlburt, *The Story of Chautauqua*, 171.

17. David Taylor, *Guide Book to Palestine Park* (Chautauqua, NY: Chautauqua Institution, 1936) 5.

18. Lenny Ben-David, *American Interests in the Holy Land Revealed in Early Photographs from 1840 to 1940* (Jerusalem: Urim Publications, 2017); Davis, *Landscapes of Belief*; Long, *Imagining the Holy Land*; Stephanie Stidham Rogers, *Inventing the Holy Land: American Protestant Pilgrimage to Palestine, 1865–1941* (Lanham MD: Lexington Books, 2011); Lester Irwin Vogel, *To See a Promised Land: American and the Holy Land in the Nineteenth Century* (University Park: Pennsylvania State University Press, 1993); and Brian Yothers, *The Romance of the Holy Land in American Travel Writing, 1790–1876* (Aldershot, England: Ashgate, 2007).

19. Long, *Imagining the Holy Land*, 1.

20. Long, *Imagining the Holy Land*, 4.

21. Jill Stevenson, *Sensational Devotion: Evangelical Performance in Twenty-First-Century America* (Ann Arbor: University of Michigan Press, 2013).

22. John Fletcher, *Preaching to Convert: Evangelical Outreach and Performance Activism in a Secular Age* (Ann Arbor: University of Michigan Press, 2013).

23. Kristin Dombek, "Murder in the Theme Park: Evangelical Animals and the End of the World," *TDR: Drama Review* 51, no. 1 (2007): 138–53.

24. Long, *Imagining the Holy Land*, 11.

25. Leon H. Vincent, *John Heyl Vincent: A Biographical Sketch* (New York: Macmillan, 1925), 77–78.

26. Kate F. Kimball, "Leaves from the Life of Bishop John H. Vincent. I. The Palestine Class: A Unique Experiment in Pedagogy," *Chautauquan* 72, no. 14 (December 6, 1913): 277.

27. "Fair Point," *Chautauqua Assembly Daily Herald*, 2.

28. "For the Assembly Herald," *Chautauqua Assembly Herald* 3, no. 8 (August 10, 1878): 5.

29. "The Sunday School," *Chautauqua Assembly Herald* 22, Advance #1 (June 1897): 11.

30. Bert O. States, *Great Reckonings in Little Rooms: On the Phenomenology of Theatre* (Berkeley: University of California Press, 1985).

31. "The Point," *Chautauqua Assembly Herald* 8, no. 4 (August 8, 1883): 1.

32. "Fair Point, or the Story of Miss Ida Norton at Chautauqua," *Chautauqua Assembly Daily Herald* 2, no. 11 (August 16, 1877): 4.

33. Barush, "The Root of the Route," 75.

34. Hermann Kern, *Through the Labyrinth: Designs and Meanings over 5,000 Years* (Munich: Prestel, 2000).

35. Long, *Imagining the Holy Land*, 1.

36. Bielo, *Materializing the Bible*, 28.

37. John Heyl Vincent, "Introduction," in *Bible Atlas: A Manual of Biblical Geography and History*, Jesse L. Hurlburt (Chicago: Rand, McNally & Company Publishers, 1899), v.

38. "Lessons in Orientalism," *Chautauqua Assembly Herald* 5, no. 17 (August 17, 1880): 1.

39. Edward W. Said, *Orientalism* (New York: Vintage Books, 1979), 1.

40. "Oriental Group on Palestine Park—Fairpoint," ca. 1876, Stereo View on 7"×4" card frame, Chautauqua Institution Archives.

41. "Lessons in Orientalism," *Chautauqua Assembly Herald*, 1.

42. "Anniversary Address," *Chautauqua Assembly Herald* 24, no. 23 (August 3, 1899): 6.

43. Andrew Chamberlin, *The Chautauqua Moment: Protestants, Progressives, and the Culture of Modern Liberalism* (New York: Columbia University Press, 2003), 155.

44. Hurlburt, *Story of Chautauqua*, 66–67.

45. "August O. Van Lennep," *Chautauqua Assembly Herald* 9, no. 10 (August 13, 1884): 2.

46. Long, *Imagining the Holy Land*, 27.

47. Jim Zarroli, "Chautauqua Institution Re-Examines Security after Salman Rushdie Attack," *Morning Edition*, NPR (website), August 31, 2022.

48. "Old Chautauqua Days: Through the Eye to the Mind," *Chautauquan* 13, no. 5 (August 1891): 576.

49. Hurlburt, *The Story of Chautauqua*, 47.

50. Bielo, *Materializing the Bible*.

51. "The Shrine of Christ's Passion: Come Take the Journey" (St. John, IN: Shrine of Christ's Passion, 2016); "Visit the Holy Land in Virtual Reality" (Eureka Springs, AK: Great Passion Play, 2022).

Subculture or Pop Culture?

Theatre, Fashion, and Air Guitar

Kyla Kazuschyk

THEATRE CAN FUNCTION as both a lens and a mirror, reflecting humanity and offering new perspectives through which to view the world. A work of theatre can be set within a certain subculture and, in so being, shine a light on that group and bring ideas to a wider audience. The costumes that characters wear help to tell the story and express who the characters are. In the case of *Airness*, a play about air guitar culture, the subculture highlighted in the play and the story told by the characters in costume offer new ways to look at theatre itself. Air guitar is similar to theatre: It is a new form of theatrical storytelling; it uses costume, character, and movement to tell stories; and it can inspire theatre practitioners to tell stories in engaging ways.

Other plays about subcultures use the framework of the culture to tell stories that resonate with audiences. *She Kills Monsters* uses the framework of Dungeons & Dragons (D&D) to explore themes of grief, sexuality, and belonging. The tabletop role-playing game community has grown significantly since D&D was introduced in 1974 and saw a significant jump in popularity during the COVID-19 pandemic.[1] Yet, even with this gradual growth, there are still people who are being introduced to the game for the first time when they go to see (or watch on Zoom) a production of *She Kills Monsters*. People who already play D&D might identify with characters and themes in the play even more quickly, as they see parts of themselves represented onstage. Likewise, new plays like *The Wolves* and *High School Coven* tell stories with universal themes through the lenses of the subculture communities in each play. *The Wolves* is about a women's indoor soccer league. *High School Coven* is about students interested in witchcraft. These stories will resonate immediately with people who are already members of these communities. For people who are not familiar with these subcultures, the plays bring the ideas from the communities to a wider audience. The costumes that characters wear, like soccer uniforms or goth-inspired looks, clearly communicate who the characters are. Some people who come to see a production of *The Wolves* wear warm up jackets and breakaway track pants to later attend soccer practices of their own. When they see performers onstage wearing garments similar to things they have worn, they can identify with the characters quickly. Someone who practices witchcraft and belongs to a coven might see a character onstage in the play *High School Coven* wearing a black dress and silver jewelry and think, "Oh, I have worn an outfit just like that. This character is just like me." For audience members who have not participated in soccer leagues or covens, the costumes the characters wear are a way to start communicating who the characters are and illustrating the story they are telling.

Similarly, costumes are vital to effective storytelling in Chelsea Marcantel's play *Airness*. *Airness* is about finding yourself and building confidence through competing in an air guitar championship. *Airness* sheds light on a popular subculture that itself inherently has elements of the theatrical. In the world of competitive air guitar, people develop their own characters and express their characters through dress and performance. The costumes that individuals design and create are integral to their success and enjoyment and have been since the beginning of organized air guitar competitions.

Smithsonian magazine traces the origins of the practice of air guitar back to Joe Cocker's performance at Woodstock in 1969. Though that probably wasn't the first time someone had pantomimed playing a musical instrument, it was a notable first recording.[2] As performing air guitar became more and more popular, people organized competitions to showcase and celebrate each other's work. Judges award performers scores in the style of figure skating competitions, giving points between 4.0 and 6.0 in each of the following categories: technical merit, stage presence, and "airness." "Airness" is a transcendent quality that is at once difficult to define and so crucial that an entire play was written about it.

The play *Airness*, like other plays about subcultural communities, is about figuring out how to express yourself and finding a group where you feel like you belong. Some aspects of the play are based on events in playwright Chelsea Marcantel's life. Marcantel was dating someone who got into air guitar, and at first, she didn't understand the appeal. Later, after researching the air guitar scene, she realized its parallel to her own life. She explains: "He must have felt when he found the air guitar community what I must have felt when I found the theater kids."[3] It is that same feeling of finding a community where you belong. Community can be found in theatre and in air guitar. When viewing the DC premiere of *Airness* in 2019, a reviewer also found connections to *She Kills Monsters*, observing: "While wildly different, both works center a group of misfits who find connection and escape from their everyday lives in a world suffused with fantasy. Both also give credence to author Sarah Vowell's assertion in her book *The Partly Cloudy Patriot* that 'being a nerd, which is to say going too far and caring too much about a subject, is the best way to make friends I know.'"[4] Air guitar, Dungeons & Dragons, and theatre are all places where people can escape their daily lives and find connection in fun fantasy worlds. By being the fullest extension of yourself, you are able to connect with others who are being the fullest extensions of themselves. When you care passionately about something, you can easily connect with other people who care passionately about the same thing. This happens in tabletop role-playing game communities and is portrayed in the play *She Kills Monsters*. This also happens in air guitar and is portrayed in the play *Airness*.

In the world of competitive air guitar, character development is key, much as it is in theatre. Theatre and air guitar share altruistic goals. The purpose of theatre is to teach and to entertain. According to their official website, "The purpose of the Air Guitar World Championships is to promote world peace." Organizers believe that since you literally cannot hold a gun while you are holding an air guitar, "wars will end, climate change will stop and all bad things will vanish when all the people in the world play the air guitar."[5] Air guitarist Matt Burns, aka Airistotle, explains that the world championship began when a group of college students in Finland were given the homework assignment to devise possible ways to achieve world peace.[6]

To create this peace through entertainment, participants start by inventing an onstage persona. People develop characters with entire backstories and distinctive personalities and express those characters through costume and movement. Justin Howard, aka Nordic Thunder, said of the infinite possibilities and potential contained in air guitar: "Creating your air-guitar character is an opportunity to be anything you want."[7] You get to express who you are through the way you move onstage and the clothes you wear onstage, just like in theatre. You can be anything, from a character who wears spandex leggings and T-shirts of heavy metal bands to a character who wears poufy dresses and devil horns.

In theatre, characters are usually dictated by the script, while in air guitar, performers entirely create their own characters. Airistotle talks about how he developed his persona, saying that while most air guitarists represent a heavy metal background and aesthetic, because he grew up listening to more punk bands like Green Day, his look represents that: an exaggerated version of the class clown, coming straight to the stage from after-school detention. He wears brightly colored trousers, fitted baseball caps, sometimes a tank top featuring the stoned sun logo of the southern California reggae/punk band Sublime.[8] In a *Sports Illustrated* profile, Airistotle describes his initial reaction to air guitar, which he found to be an intriguing mix of comedy show, concert, and sporting event: "It's like a drag show, but for frat bros."[9] Air guitar combines elements of drag, such as dressing up and moving onstage to music, and presents them in a way that reaches communities drag might not reach. People who attend and participate in drag shows are often, though not always, people who identify as queer, trans, gay, nonbinary, gender fluid, or are otherwise on the LGBTQIA spectrum. Drag shows can be overexaggerated performances of gender, sometimes by people who present as masculine presenting as feminine. The "frat bros" that Airistotle is referring to might be people who have not attended gay bars or nightclubs where drag shows take place. For straight, cis men, it can seem unacceptable to express yourself through costumes and dance, yet air guitar creates a space where this is celebrated. In air guitar, you can invent a character and then perform as that character. The name you choose, the way you move onstage, and the clothes you wear onstage convey that character to the audience.

The name, choreography, and costumes that Matt Burns uses in his air guitar performances help him to express himself and connect with his community. Burns chose the name "Airistotle" for his air guitar pseudonym perhaps in part because he "firmly believes that a performance must have a beginning, a middle and an end." His name is a nod to the philosopher Aristotle, who is credited with establishing the commonly followed story structure of rising action, climax, and falling action. When Airistotle first won the US Air Guitar competition, organizer Kriston Rucker remarked that his work was elevating the sport of air guitar by paying close attention to elements of performance including "character coherence, 60-second story arc, the power of entrance," and "how to rope-a-dope the crowd with faux vulnerability, et cetera."[10] The elements of performance in air guitar are almost exactly the same as in traditional theatre. Both involve an arc of story structure, character coherence, making an entrance, and engaging an audience.

While Burns's Airistotle is an exaggerated version of himself, his friend Mike Katz created a character, Brozone Layer, a "fratty tough guy," who is the opposite of who he is in real life. Some performers take their characters very seriously. Rob Weychert, aka Windhammer, who appears shirtless and in dark leather pants, never smiles while onstage, a foil to the cheerful and colorful Airistotle.[11] Whether personas are extensions of or opposites to ourselves, the costumes they wear and the way they move onstage are important to telling their stories. Characters in the play *Airness* reflect this spectrum; some performers' onstage personas are an extension of their real-life personas and others are quite different from who they are offstage.

When working on the role of Nina in a production of *Airness*, actor Jerrie Johnson formed this perspective on air guitar personas: "Either personas (are) a completely different version of yourself—sweet guys playing crazy rock gods—or it's the person you want to be or the things you want to see, so it's like a heightened version of yourself."[12] Air guitarists like Brozone Layer and Mean Melin are portraying characters that are the opposite of who they are in real life, whereas Airistotle and Mom Jeans Jeanie are playing characters that are heightening and enhancing aspects of their own personalities. Cannibal

Queen is taking one aspect of herself and amplifying and exaggerating it to become her persona, while Shreddy Eddy is being the most authentic version of himself.

Using a persona to tell a story is similar in air guitar and in professional wrestling, both of which are forms of theatre. In theatre, performers embody characters that are written in a script. In professional wrestling and in air guitar, performers embody personas that they invent themselves. Kriston Rucker, an organizer with the United States Air Guitar national organization makes the comparison to professional wrestling: "If American wrestling didn't exist and someone said, 'What if grown men wore leotards and pretended to fight?' it would sound ridiculous. . . . But no one gives it a thought now."[13] As professional wrestling has grown in popularity, it has become more acceptable as a way to watch people tell stories on a stage, just like air guitar.

The similarities between air guitar and professional wrestling become even more apparent in one of Airistotle's performances. WWE's The Undertaker is known for making a dramatic entrance, prefaced by ominous music and a spotlight shining on his black leather cowboy hat sitting in the middle of the ring. In Airistotle's version, a spotlight shines on his hat sitting onstage, a light blue, flat brim baseball hat embroidered with Nickelodeon's Rocko the wallaby, a cartoon character Barnes loved when he was young.[14] Wrestling fans in the audience who have seen the Undertaker in any of the hundreds of wrestling competitions he has performed in will probably understand the reference. They will recognize the music they have heard before and the staging of a light shining on a hat. When the Undertaker enters the arena, the mood is ominous and foreboding. He is a character that dresses all in black and scowls a lot. Wrestling fans who have seen the Undertaker perform might hear the music and expect something dark and mysterious, becoming surprised and amused when instead they see Airistotle. His costumes are brightly colored and his expression is cheerful, a drastic difference from those of the Undertaker. Taking something scary and making it silly by changing costumes and movement is one way to engage audiences.

Air guitar competitions often bridge the divide between performer and audience. Beth Melin, aka CindAirella describes how competitions in Lawrence, Kansas, conclude with everyone in the space, performers and spectators, being invited to the stage to play air guitar to the classic Lynyrd Skynyrd jam "Free Bird."[15] In *Airness*, the character of Facebender speaks of the vitality of the audience, saying, "the life of the spectator and the life of the performer are two halves of the same whole. You cannot fully appreciate one without the other."[16] In a conversation with Alex Forbes, aka Ricky Stinkfingers, a Brooklyn Paper writer wonders who is having more fun: the performers or their legions of fans?[17] The distance between performers and audience members collapses. We are all spectators and we are all performing something, and we are all here together. As Golden Thunder says in *Airness*, "Air guitar is not about OR, it's about AND." Air guitar's way of connecting performers and audiences can inspire traditional theatre to find that same connection. In a production of *Airness* at Louisiana State University, performers onstage invited the audience to cheer and boo and stand up and play air guitar along to "Freebird" at the end. Theatre can be fun, and it can tell stories in all kinds of different ways. Theatre can inspire you to be yourself in community with other people.

Air guitar can be a way to be the fullest version of yourself or to amplify parts of yourself that are otherwise silenced. For people who identify as women, a feeling of having to carry a shield to be safe in the world can be pervasive. A space where you can safely express power, darkness, sensuality, eccentricity, silliness, or anything else can be vitally restorative. Brittany Diaz, aka Georgia Lunch, describes her onstage persona as "a version of me when I don't give a fuck."[18] In daily life, Brittany often wears denim shorts and black band T-shirts. To transform into Georgia Lunch, she adds leggings printed with lightning bolts or skulls and black fishnet sleeves. The improved self-image and self-confidence Diaz attributes to air guitar may have been the inspiration for the character of Cannibal Queen in *Airness*. Cannibal Queen talks about how she feels like she must carry a shield to be safe in the world, but, she says, "When I get up on stage, I can put my shield down and let all my darkness come rushing out."[19] Cannibal Queen is a heel character, a character designed for audiences to love to hate. When I designed costumes for *Airness*, I made Cannibal Queen a crown of skulls, black roses, and black rhinestones. I dressed her all in black, with black platform boots and a tank top with a pentagram on it. I make her a feather boa to drape around her shoulders, but instead of being made out of feathers, it was made out of plastic skulls. She wore the crown and the boa for the moments in the play when she was performing air guitar, at the most exaggerated version of her darkness.

Another take on a heel character in air guitar competitions is Mom Jeans Jeanie. Nicole Sevcik, aka Mom Jeans Jeanie, has also created a character that is an exaggerated extension of real-life self. As she is getting dressed for a competition, her children running around at her feet, she explains, "Part of transforming is this wig. She is fifty percent blonde hair. This outfit is the other fifty percent." Mom Jeans Jeanie wears high-waisted blue jeans, blouses with sweater vests, and a short blonde wig.[20] She demonstrates who her character is through the costumes she wears and the way she moves onstage. In a performance at the world championship in 2017, Mom Jeans Jeanie enters the stage smiling sweetly and holding a large book. She turns the book around to reveal the title to the audience: "Don't Talk to Strangers." She shakes her head no and wags her finger, still smiling. Then she opens the book, reaches inside, pulls out a handful of confetti, and throws it in the air as the music starts, a rock song blaring "Don't talk to strangers!" She throws the book down, moves her arms and legs to the music, growing more and more frantic, her facial expression an intense grimace. She pantomimes playing the guitar behind her head, she lunges, her movements get bigger and wider as the music swells, she twirls around and the song ends. She picks up the book and smiles sweetly again, bashfully waving off the crowd's applause.[21] Whether you are a director staging a play or an air guitar player preparing a performance, you've got to think about blocking, how you move on the stage. As in dance, routines are often meticulously choreographed. Other times, air guitarists move in a spontaneous way, like actors when they are improvising a scene. Mean Melin compares air guitar directly to theatre, saying, "Your one-minute competition song is like a three-act play. You're telling a story with your whole body."[22]

Telling a story with your whole body through gestures accompanied by music can also be defined as pantomime. Miming is telling the audience a story involving an object without using an actual physical object. Mimes act as if an invisible object is there, just as the air guitarist plays an invisible guitar. Ethnomusicologist (and air guitar champion) Byrd McDaniel draws parallels through the history of pantomimed musical performances, highlighting how lip syncing

> became an enduring feature of drag performance in LGBTQ subcultures, where performers would simulate singing to recorded music as a cheaper alternative to hiring live musicians. Beyond the humorous, ironic façade of these performances is a sincere craft that has exploded in popularity over the past couple of decades. . . . Air guitar playing was goofy. It was energetic. And it was fun. But it was also a way to sincerely engage with music. It allowed manly men to move their bodies to music, while avoiding gendered stereotypes that dancing should be something feminine and unmanly.[23]

Air guitar is like drag because there is recorded music playing and a performer is moving to the music to entertain an audience. In both performances, performers are often warmly supported by audiences and cheered on for expressing any performance of gender along the gender spectrum. The costumes they wear and the way they move tell the audience who they are presenting. Spaces like these, where people of all gender identities can feel comfortable and supported by a community while openly performing femininity or masculinity, are rare and precious. People who participate in air guitar competitions are deliberately creating communities that are welcoming. Air guitarists can encourage and support each other, just as theatre artists can.

In *Airness*, veteran air guitarist Shreddy Eddy is welcoming newcomer Nina to the community. He tries to explain to her that air guitar "comes from a time before you cared about looking cool."[24] As Nina grows in self-awareness and self-confidence throughout the play, her costumes reflect this loss of inhibitions. When I designed costumes for a production of *Airness* at Louisiana State University in 2022, I styled Nina in casual gray and black for her first appearance onstage. She wears gray cutoff shorts over black fishnet tights, a gray tank top, and a black hoodie. Nina talks about how she is in an actual band and looks down on air guitar. As she becomes friends with the air guitarists and learns more about the sport and the culture surrounding it, she learns to accept herself and feels more comfortable expressing parts of herself that she had been hiding or had forgotten about since she was a child, like her unadulterated passion for rock and roll. Little by little, throughout the play, she adds more brightly colored garments and accessories. When we see her perform her air guitar routine at the end of the play, she wears zebra print, flared trousers, a sparkly teal top, a hot pink blazer, and lime-green fingerless gloves. Costumes help to communicate to the audience who the characters are, both in scripted plays and in air guitar competitions.

Costumes are important in theatre, and they are especially important in air guitar. In traditional theatre, the telling of the story and the expression of characters is supported by costumes as well as by scenery, props, lighting, and sound. Air guitar competitions happen in spaces that are often music venues, nightclubs, or bars. Sometimes there is a stage, yet there is no scenery on the stage, no set to indicate location. Sometimes there is preprogrammed lighting to enhance the show, and often it is the same basic lighting setup for each performer. The sound of the music the air guitarist is playing along to is important, of course. The absence of the prop of the guitar is, as mentioned, what defines the form. So, the remaining theatrical element is perhaps the most vital: the costumes. Costumes are critical to the success and enjoyment of both the air guitarists and the audience. Standout costumes can mean the difference between winning and losing competitions. A performer's costume is what tells the audience who their character is. Costumes help performers grow in confidence, and fantastic costumes bring joy to performers and audiences alike. This is true both for air guitar competitions and for more traditional theatre.

Whether creating costumes for theatre or for air guitar competitions, which can be seen as a new form of theatre, reflecting trends in fashion and in makeup is crucial to creating authentic characters. Costume designer Mary Eggers spoke about her work on a 2018 production of *Airness* at the Chautauqua Theater Company, saying: "You sort of have to approach it like a period show because these people exist. . . . You have to do the actual people research and learn as much as you can without being in the world before you feel comfortable putting clothes on (actors) and feeling authentic."²⁵ Authentic characters are key to connecting with an audience, and costumes can enhance this authenticity.

In one scene in *Airness*, a character's costumes are described in detail. When Golden Thunder performs, he peels off one outer layer to reveal a shirt with "Make Air Not War" written in sequins across the chest. Then, to the music of Billy Idol's "Rebel Yell," he takes off his trousers to reveal boxer shorts that are half union flag, half confederate flag, eventually ripping those in half to reveal American flag briefs.²⁶ Other characters in the play criticize Golden Thunder, saying his message doesn't come across. Though invoking Union, Confederate, and American flags to make a statement about the importance of unity might be unclear, the message of his sequined T-shirt is strong. "Make Air Not War," a play on the anti-war slogan "Make Love Not War," is another way to express the goal of the international air guitar competition, the idea that we can achieve world peace through air guitar because you can't hold a gun while you are holding an air guitar.

The lines in the play articulate the ephemeral beauty of air guitar and theatre. The character Facebender tells Nina about his gruesome day job cleaning up murder scenes and then says: "I look death in its nasty face every day. And then at night, I come here, and I get up onstage and live like there's no tomorrow. Because there isn't. There really isn't. It's silly and it's fun and it's absurd, but life is a slow march off a cliff into nothingness, so why not be as silly as you want?"²⁷ When the character Facebender is saying these lines, he is articulating the idea of expressing yourself freely and being welcomed and supported by a community. This can happen both in air guitar and in theatre.

The air guitar world championship, held every summer in Oulu, Finland, has grown into an event far larger than many nights of theatre. Covering this event, reporter Anupama Khedkar observed: "Air guitaring is a passion, an activity no longer associated with the enthusiastic metal fan anymore. It's got a massive fan base and a festival that kicks ass. Every year, several thousand people gather to watch these rock n roll loving folks shred air guitars onstage—lip-syncing, exaggerated hand movement, head-banging and all. They spend hours of their time practicing the perfect routine that ultimately lasts only a few minutes."²⁸ This is not unlike the hours/days/weeks/months we put into creating characters onstage in the theatre. Both deal in ephemeral beauty. Khedkar's conclusions are similar to those often drawn about community theatre: "Amazingly, this festival encompasses much more than the ability to play an invisible guitar, there's a whole mutual respect in the community that's vaguely comforting. Everybody adores and respects the air guitar."²⁹ Like theatre, air guitar is a community of people who accept each other for who they are.

Charlotte Wilder for *Sports Illustrated* could have been describing live theatre when she said of watching the air guitar championships: "You will not understand this until you see it live. There's just no way. I'm doing my best to describe it, and you can watch videos, but until you witness this in person you will not *feel the airness*."[30] In the same way, film and television and even Zoom performance cannot match the energy felt in live theatre.

Notes

1. Sarah Whitten, "Dungeons & Dragons Had Its Biggest Year Ever as COVID Forced the Game Off Tables and Onto the Web," CNBC (website), March 13, 2021, accessed February 21, 2022.

2. April White, "An Electrifying History of Air Guitar: How the World's Most Popular Invisible Instrument Became Such a Hit," *Smithsonian* (website), July 2019, accessed August 23, 2022.

3. Kevin C. Vestsal, "In 'Airness,' Playwright Chelsea Marcantel Strives for Authentic Presentation of Unfamiliar Form," Chautauquan Daily (website), July 18, 2018, accessed February 21, 2022.

4. John Bavoso, "Review: Airness. An Air Guitar Comedy Whose Wildly Talented Cast Strikes a Comedy Chord," DC Theatre Scene (website), November 19, 2019, accessed March 15, 2022.

5. "Story," Air Guitar World Championships (website), accessed March 15, 2022.

6. "Vice Specials: Air Guitar Championship." Vice Video (website), accessed February 21, 2022.

7. Allison Babka, "Guitar Zero: The Search Is on for St. Louis' Air Apparent," Riverfront Times (website), June 27, 2013, accessed March 14, 2022.

8. "Vice Specials: Air Guitar Championship." Vice Video.

9. Charlotte Wilder, "Matt 'Aristotle' Burns and the U.S. Air Guitar Championships Will Rock Your World," *Sports Illustrated* (website), August 22, 2018, accessed February 21, 2022.

10. Wilder, "Matt 'Aristotle' Burns and the U.S. Air Guitar Championships Will Rock Your World."

11. Wilder, "Matt 'Aristotle' Burns and the U.S. Air Guitar Championships Will Rock Your World."

12. Kevin C. Vestal, "'Airness' Costume Designer Eggers Crafts Heightened On-Stage Personas," Chautauquan Daily (website), July 20, 2018, accessed February 21, 2022.

13. Allison Babka, "Guitar Zero: The Search Is on for St. Louis' Air Apparent," Riverfront Times (website), June 27, 2013, accessed March 14, 2022.

14. Wilder, "Matt 'Aristotle' Burns and the U.S. Air Guitar Championships Will Rock Your World."

15. Fally Afani, "Embracing Silliness: How the U.S. Air Guitar Competition

Flourished in Lawrence," I Heart Local Music (website), April 25, 2017

16. Chelsea Marcantel, *Airness* (New York: Playscripts, 2019).

17. Daniel Ng, "Air Apparent! Fake Guitar Championships Are Back." Brooklyn Paper (website), June 8, 2011, accessed February 21, 2022.

18. "Vice Specials: Air Guitar Championship." Vice Video.

19. Marcantel, *Airness*.

20. "Vice Specials: Air Guitar Championship." Vice Video.

21. Nicole "Mom Jeans Jeanie" Sevcik (USA) 2017 Air Guitar World Championships, YouTube (website), August 26, 2017, accessed August 29, 2022.

22. Babka, "Guitar Zero: The Search Is on for St. Louis' Air Apparent."

23. Byrd McDaniel, "How Air Guitar Became a Serious Sport," Conversation (website), April 29, 2019, accessed February 21, 2022.

24. Marcantel, *Airness*.

25. Vestal, "'Airness' Costume Designer Eggers Crafts Heightened On-Stage Personas."

26. Marcantel, *Airness*.

27. Marcantel, *Airness*.

28. Anupama Khedkar, "Here's Everything You Need to Know About the Air Guitar World Championship." Sherpaland (website), August 19, 2015, accessed February 21, 2022.

29. Khedkar, "Here's Everything You Need to Know About the Air Guitar World Championship."

30. Wilder, "Matt 'Aristotle' Burns and the U.S. Air Guitar Championships Will Rock Your World."

Staging Black Popularity

One Night in Miami and the Historic Hampton House

Mysia Anderson

ONE NIGHT IN *Miami* (2013) is a narrative animated by spectacular Black figures of the Jim Crow period. Written by Kemp Powers, this fictional account begins on an evening of destiny—the night twenty-two-year-old Cassius Clay ascended to legendary status by winning the 1964 heavyweight title. Rather than showcasing this opening visual, the stage directions gesture toward sonic flashes of Clay's crowning: "We hear [Cassius] say how he's the greatest and shook up the world. We hear him invite Sam Cooke into the ring. The noise builds to deafening levels before dropping into complete [Silence]."[1] Silence performs a theatrical reorientation into the play's central setting, Black Miami's Hampton House. Inside the Miami Beach Convention Hall, the cheering crowd lionized Clay as a young champion, though outside the ring's glory, Black people were prohibited from the surrounding tourist paradise. People of African descent could travel to the Miami Beach area only for work and were required to carry physical ID passes.[2] Located miles away from the fight, the Hampton House—an integrated Green Book hotel—welcomed the night's Black celebration. In *Overground Railroad: The Green Book and the Roots of Black Travel in America*, Candacy Taylor explicates how the Green Book, one of several Black travel guides responding to the Jim Crow period, offered Black travelers "courage and security"[3] by charting Black-owned and Black-friendly businesses. The Green Book pinpointed where Black motorists could find gas, entertainment, food, lodging, and luxury.

The Hampton House, founded by a white Jewish couple named Harry and Florence Markowitz, garnered a reputation as a luxurious Green Book–approved hotel. It boasted fifty rooms, a twenty-four-hour restaurant, a nightclub, and a swimming pool, attracting wealthy Black patrons. With an iron double staircase anchoring the check-in desk, it grandly displayed Mediterranean architecture and offered air-conditioned rooms to characteristically well-dressed guests. However, *One Night in Miami* chooses to omit the grandeur of this opulent setting. It focuses on the intimate moments following the fervor of triumph, and the entirety of the play occurs within the boundaries of a private room. The play stewards an intimate space for Cassius Clay, Malcolm X, Sam Cooke, and Jim Brown to examine the psychological effects of racism, share secrets, reveal their desires, investigate shared upbringings, and counsel each other about their places in the struggle for liberation.

Powers stages intimate encounters of a probable yet unconfirmed exchange. It is rumored that all men were present in Miami on that night; some of them were even photographed in the "Gentlemen's Room" at the Hampton House. A central allure of the story is the probability that this conversation happened at that moment in time, just as it is happening for audiences contemporarily. As such, Powers's world-making dwells in the possibility of intimacy that the Hampton House was able to provide Black travelers in anti-Black landscapes. This singular room is more than a symbolic spatial representation of the Jim Crow period. The confined space transforms into a crossroads for the men shaping the popular during a pivotal time in American history. Surrounded by the walls of a Green Book hotel, they are held within an off-the-record space, absent of televisions, radios, reporters, fans, and families, to candidly examine, share, and defend aspects of their public and interior lives. Stephen Best describes the ontology of historical rumor as "an appearance made possible only in its disappearance; an aspiration registered at the moment of its suppression; a power that reaffirms itself by liquidating its sources."[4] Best argues that rumors and archives reaffirm each other. Rumor needs the archive to plant speculative seeds; the archive needs rumor to confirm its authority. While pictures captured a few of the men in the Hampton House that night, there are no hotel ledgers to confirm their presence. In the case of this story, the reliance on rumor is tied to racialized property relations. Twelve years after the possibility of this conversation, the Hampton House was abandoned with the dawn of integration.

Deserted by 1976, the Hampton House was defenseless against hurricanes, storms, wildlife, and erasure. In the early 2000s, Miami-Dade County was set on tearing the Hampton House down. The Hampton House was built in the Brownsville community. N. D. B. Connolly's *A World More Concrete: Real Estate and the Remaking of Jim Crow South Florida* analyzes this locale's history as a racially contested geography. Settled in the twentieth century, Brownsville was an all-white, rural patch of land registered as the Brown Subdivision. After World War II, an influx of upwardly mobile people of color began buying homes in the area, prompting displays of cross burnings, marches, and other forms of white supremacist terrorism. As people of color who were in search of the promise of homeownership, these new Brownsville residents actively resisted racial zoning by collectively organizing and successfully appealing to the Florida Supreme Court. Yet, the compounding white flight and racial animosity transformed Brown Sub into a social pariah that was to be punished through municipal disdain. Connolly explains how Brownsville residents, like many homeowners in Black Miami, experienced being denied permits for home improvements, predatory policing, insufficient city services, price gouging, and a litany of other anti-Black property relations. The Markowitz couple invested in the Hampton House during a time of economic possibility, as they were inspired by the hopes and desires of the surrounding upwardly mobile community. Although they hoped to attract wealthy African Americans visiting Miami, the structural divestment of Brownsville impacted their business—especially once wealthy people of color were legally permitted to stay in Miami Beach establishments.[5]

Unrecognizable according to those early ambitions, the Hampton House of the 2000s had transformed into a site that housed homeless communities, addicts, drug dealers, and sex workers. Due to the stereotypes and social neglect weaponized against these socially marked identities in the city, the Hampton House was tethered to disposability. The current owner grew weary of complaints from neighbors and sold the property to the county. It was then that a resident of the community, a Black educator and historical preservationist named Enid Pinkney, rallied political imagination, performance, and celebrity memory to lead a mission to save the remnants of Hampton House. Although the county could not see the potential of the space and divested from its history, she remembered the Hampton House when it was "quite an elegant place."[6] Pinkney was the leading voice in stopping the demolition, and her memories of another time rooted the Hampton House's rehabilitation in the communal arts organization that it is today.

Candacy Taylor, a contemporary photographer and cultural documentarian, confessed that the Hampton House has "lost its shine."[7] In its former glory, this hotel was a place where Aretha Franklin and Sammy Davis Jr. would sing legendary melodies in one room before laying their heads in another. Taylor encountered the Hampton House decades after the glitz and glamour of yesteryear. It now stood as a cultural landmark with a history marked by abandonment. Over the course of a three-year expedition to nearly five thousand Green Book sites, Taylor found that less than 5 percent of the establishments are still in existence. She states, "in less than a decade after the passage of the Civil Rights Act, at least half of the Green Book Black-owned businesses were closed, either through lack of support or through eminent domain, which allowed federal, state, and city governments to take over the land to expand freeway systems and for urban renewal projects."[8] Taylor contends that there is a correlation between the divestment of the sites and national divestment of Black communities. She writes:

While photographing the Hampton House in Miami and patiently waiting for a young prostitute, naked from the waist down, to walk out of my frame, I realized I wasn't interested in presenting the Green Book as a historic time capsule. I wanted to show it in the context of this country's ongoing struggle with race and social mobility, because the problems black Americans face regarding police brutality, homicide, unfair drug sentencing, and mass incarceration are arguably just as debilitating and deadly as the problems the Green Book helped black people avoid more than eighty years ago.[9]

Before Pinkney's vision, the Hampton House nearly had the same fate as the majority of Green Book businesses. Many of them now serve as tombstones for beloved places that once held Black life, and their histories illuminate the vulnerability of Black futurity. Juxtaposing the Hampton House's contemporary presentation with the luminescence of the past, Taylor's visitation bears witness to the structural negligence of Black Miamian geographies of the past, present, and future. As Taylor demonstrates, these sites are geographic and temporal markers that capture the waning of departed Black world-making. Their loss of popularity heralded a new lived reality, but the memories of the past still lived on through the people who recall a different moment. Jonathan Scott Holloway's *Jim Crow Wisdom: Memory and Identity in Black America since 1940* parses out the sea of questions that lies in between memory and archival authority.[10] For Holloway, "the literal truth is less important . . . than the act of remembrance itself. This is the act that shapes consciousness and an identity, and this is the act that [he finds] most compelling in telling stories about the black past."[11] While Holloway is primarily concerned with how violence is critical to the formation of Black identity and memory, the Hampton House recuperation also gestures to the power of the popular—and the fabulous—in shaping Black memory.

As the founder of the restored site, Pinkney activated the power of uplifting memories, and she countered financial barriers by mobilizing performative displays of popularity. Relying on an entanglement of Black visual culture and social mobility, her tactics for saving the Hampton House share a confluence with the Hampton House's most visible representation, *One Night in Miami*. This play-turned-movie frames an examination of the political capacity of Black popularity in the struggle for Black sustainability. The power of the popular, widely circulated, and beloved cultural artifacts, aesthetics, images, emotions, and ideas is interrogated within the racial confinement experienced by socially mobile Black men. Whether intentional or not, the story can serve as allegory for its larger geographic setting. From the collection of oral histories and activation of performance theory, I argue that Pinkney's journey to restoring the Hampton House and Powers's theatrical storytelling enunciate the role of Black popularity in the preservation of Black Miami history. As Stuart Hall astutely argues, the popular is often commodified, and it's a stereotyped arena seeped in mythology.[12] Woven together, the two stories critically examine the realm of popular culture in the struggle to sustainably preserve Black Miami memory when facing state neglect and economic divestment.

Pinkney's institution-building responds to the diminishment of Brownsville and Black Miami as a whole. In 2020, *Anthurium: A Caribbean Studies Journal* published an entire issue dedicated to the search of Black Miamian experiences by assembling critical research and life-writings. In the introduction, titled "Looking For Black Miami," Donnette Francis and Allison Harris frame the practice of *looking for the city* as the issue's central ethos, organizing principle, and methodology. They state, "A city built on the speculation of real estate, transportation, banking, agriculture, and tourism, Miami has only recently registered in national public policy conversations around Blackness or scholarly theorization of Black aesthetics."[13] The discursive performance of looking for Black Miami, a geographically fixed and seemingly identifiable location, underscores the city's routine absence in academic discourse, but the desire to look for the Blackness within the city moves beyond the address of a theoretical unpopularity. As the city faces environmental degradation, climate gentrification, speculative development, lack of economic opportunity, and profound violence, Black Miamian women are actively resisting reenactments of structural abandonment by cultivating acts of futurity.[14] By capturing Enid Pinkney's story in conversation with these popular depictions, I hope to contribute to an expansive representation of Black Miami history.

"Transferring" the Past

Dr. Enid Pinkney and I met on an early Saturday morning at the Historic Hampton in 2022. Her nephew, who is also her main caregiver, accompanied her to speak with me before her dialysis appointment later that afternoon. I brought along my grandmother, Betty Simon, who is eighty-one years old. During the first few years of her marriage to my grandfather James Simon, my grandmother lived in the Hampton House apartments. My grandparents met as tenants in the apartments, and after what my grandmother remembers as an uneventful date, they decided to keep seeing each other and got married soon after. Following the birth of their third daughter, my mother, they left the apartments in 1963 and became the first Black family to move onto their block. Their new neighborhood was on the side of the railroad tracks where Black families were historically unwelcomed. Their hostile neighbors put up "blockbuster" signs on their door with the intentions to both intimidate new residents of color seeking to integrate the neighborhood and to alert other white residents to their presence. My late grandfather recalled being invited to "community meetings," which he declined. My family's integration story is emblematic of other scenes that were happening all over the city as Black people sought to remap their lives into rapidly changing landscapes. This movement brought about acts of freedom that transgressed boundaries, as well as new spatial orders that resulted in communal loss. The Hampton House replica I brought my grandmother to is different from the hotel she once knew. Together, we learned about the personal histories that drove Pinkney to become an advocate for the preservation of Black Miami's history and culture.[15]

Pinkney's parents were born in the Bahamas, a vital locale in Miami's history, as both Black Bahamian and Black American men were among the 182 authorizing votes cast to incorporate the city. Pinkney and her brother were primarily raised by their grandmother and aunt because their parents lived on their "boss man's" premises in Miami Beach. Her father was a gardener, and her mother was a maid. Her parents' boss owned a plantation estate, but he lived there only during the winter months. When he and his wife came down south, they always wanted to see Pinkney and her brother. Pinkney remembers this as an exciting time because she looked forward to a rare opportunity to go to the beach. During these reunions, the "boss man" would have them recite poetry, sing songs, or perform any kind of drama they had learned. Pinkney spent her childhood playing piano and acting in plays for church, school, and community programs. These embodied practices gave her confidence and allowed her to connect with her surrounding community. Listening to her memories of entertaining her parents' employer felt outside this sphere of communal performance. For instance, Pinkney remembers the "boss man" asking her and her brother to dance. Her father refused the request and informed his boss that his children did not dance.[16]

Pinkney's father was not only a gardener but also a minister, and he built the first Holiness Church in the historically Black neighborhood known as Carver's Ranch. She said, "I love to dance, but we couldn't dance. I remember I got so scared because my father told his boss what he wasn't going to do, and this is the white man. He's talking back to the white man. I was thinking they might fire him, and during that time, that was a good job."[17] Pinkney was in elementary school when she made these critical assessments of racialized performance. She admits that by that young age, she had already been indoctrinated into segregation and had to endure its psychological effects. Commenting on contemporary times, she said, "White people don't want their children feeling guilty about what happened a long time ago, and these same people don't consider the psychological effect segregation had on Black children."[18] Throughout her childhood, her father's performance of resistive self-regard against local codes of white supremacy would become instructive to her own journey.

One evening, Pinkney and her family were driving home from church on State Road 9 when two police officers stopped them. The officers claimed that Pinkney's father was driving with bright lights and ordered him to get out of the car. When Pinkney's father got out of the car, an officer ordered him to remove his hat. She remembers her father asking what constitutional law required him to remove his hat. As Bahamian immigrants and property owners, Pinkney's parents were required to attend citizenship school at Dunbar Elementary. They thoroughly studied the constitution to become citizens and secure property tax exemptions. The police officer did not appreciate the question. He slapped her father across his face, knocking his hat off. Her father then picked up the hat and put it back on his head. Perhaps the officer envied the quality of this hat; it was an expensive Stetson hat, a gift from his "boss man." Either way, her father was right. There was no law that required him to perform submission by removing his hat. The officer then said that they were going to take him to jail for disrespecting a police officer. Her father denied this allegation and reminded the officer that he had in fact disrespected him by knocking his hat off of his head. The officer retorted that her father was now being insubordinate by talking back.[19]

The police officer then went to Pinkney's mother and asked her to help calm Pinkney's father down. Her father warned the officer not to speak to her. Instead, he ordered the officer to take him to jail immediately, so he could make a phone call to his employer. The officers took him away and left Pinkney, her mother, and her brother on the side of the road with no way of getting back home to Overtown. Although he did not have a license, Pinkney's brother knew how to drive and offered his services. She recalled her mother saying, "Between you and your daddy, y'all gon' kill me!" She knew that if the police had caught him driving, they would take him to jail too. Suddenly, the three saw a police car coming toward them. She recalls her mother thinking that they were sending a police car to see if they were still there, but it was actually the same police officers who had Pinkney's daddy in the back seat. In this situation, which seemed like a comedy trying hard to be a drama, the police officers asked him if he would consider having more respect for a police officer if they were to stop him again. Her father questioned what they meant by that and reminded them that he didn't disrespect them like they had disrespected him by slapping him so hard they knocked his hat off his head (Pinkney's mother thought she was going to die!). They told him that they were going to let him go this time, but if they caught him again, they were going to take him to jail. Of course, her father responded in kind; her mother told him to shut up and said, "Let's get out of here!"[20]

Looking back, Pinkney knows that while her family's legacy has shaped her into who she is today, she was not exempt from the psychological limitations that segregation instilled in her. She gave the example of racism's psychological impact when she recalled her trip to The Bahamas to retrace her family history after her mother's passing. After her mother died, everything she said gained more significance to Pinkney. Her mother's maiden name was Clark, and her great-great-grandmother was the child of a plantation owner who left her more than "200 acres of ocean front property and 58 slaves." Her mother used to say, "the Clarks owned oceanfront property," but Pinkney never believed her because she lived in a context where Black people could not go to the beach. The stories her mother told about "picking coco plums and going to the ocean to swim" encouraged Pinkney to visit her mother's birthplace for the first time. She wanted to walk the same roads she used to walk and to pick coco plums—"whatever those were." When she and a friend were traveling on a plane to go to the island of Great Exuma, the stewardess opened the cabin door and exposed two Black pilots who were navigating the plane. Pinkney was "so scared!" At the time, she believed, "cain't no Black people fly no plane!" Through laughter, she admitted that she got as nervous as she did when her father told his boss that his children would not dance for him. Now, at ninety years old, she says she has learned how not to fear whiteness and how to not stay in her place.[21]

Enid Pinkney's recollection of this story was filled with laughter and audible responses from me and my grandmother, both of us riveted by her vivid storytelling. Under the Hampton House's covering, we were able to find the joy within the remembrance of painful moments. The space we created together was reminiscent of intimate reflections theatricalized in *One Night in Miami*. This narrative, as well as my own coperformative witnessing of Pinkney's recollection, are performances of history. In preparation for the script, Powers studied the autobiographies, newspaper articles, and FBI files concerning each of his protagonists.[22] Reminiscent of Saidiya Hartman's method of critical fabulation, his narration process rendered stories from archival fragments. Hartman's "Venus in Two Acts" explains how writing with the intention of tethering the past, present, and future creates coeval possibilities for archival subjects.[23] Audiences become synchronous with an ephemeral cultivation of celebrity intimacy, friendship, and loving critique as a roadmap to power and politics. Their isolation creates a powerful juxtaposition between the euphoria of victory and the speculations concerning the ongoing civil rights movement. The characters embody quotidian reflections about the limits of Black American popularity, and the setting illuminates racialized underpinnings of American popular culture. This liminal space of communal gathering is entangled and upheld by the history and imagined futures of the Hampton House.

Both Powers's and Pinkney's efforts demonstrate how critical fabulation could be leveraged in restoring historic sites, theatrically and physically. Pinkney believes that "you need to know who you are, and you need to celebrate who you are." She further states, "It's more than history; it needs to be transferred and transmitted to other people. What I enjoy doing is helping people pull heritage out of themselves and letting them celebrate what they find."[24] Pinkney's theory of transference echoes performance theorist Diana Taylor's conception of "the repertoire" as an embodied orientation to ways of knowing that access cultural memory. Taylor's theory of performance—"as vital acts of transfer, transmitting social knowledge, memory, and a sense of identity"—affirms Pinkney's own meaning-making between the performances she participated in and witnessed as a Black child growing up in segregation and her own historical preservation legacy.[25] She described that she has always had a passion for history throughout her education.

After graduating from Booker T. Washington High in 1949, she received her bachelor's in social science at Talladega College in 1953. In 1967, she went on to receive her master's from Barry University. She worked as a social worker before transitioning into the Dade County Public School System. Before becoming an assistant principal, she taught history, but she said, "it got to be bigger than that." As she traveled and listened to the stories of other people, she realized the importance of giving people access to their foundations, their roots. She learned a deep respect for her own legacy, and she wanted others to feel a similar, distinct respect for themselves and the legacy their family members had built.[26]

Like a play that brings to life the possibilities of a racially subjugated past, Pinkney's activation of history is material and embodied. In the mid-1980s, Pinkney joined the Miami-Dade Heritage Trust and was elected as its first Black president in 1998. She founded the African American Committee within the trust in an effort to further uplift the contributions of African Americans. She has contributed to the preservation of eleven historic sites, including the Historic Hampton House. As Diana Taylor argues, performance can constitute a methodological lens for examining events, objects, and identity.[27] Analyzing Pinkney's efforts "as performance" aligns with Pinkney's own views of how the preservation of historically significant sites performs racial uplift. This political performance strategy inevitably enters into conversation with the popular and, ultimately, the politics of representation. Powers gestures toward this relationship when he employs intimate conversations between distinguished Black men to interrogate their strategic negotiations of high visibility. When Malcolm X is questioned on his use of incendiary language on television, Clay gestures to the contradictory nature of X's private vulnerability despite his public strength. Additionally, X pesters Sam Cooke to use his musical stardom to push the movement forward, and he questions him on why he performs in segregated places on Miami Beach. In the creation of Black cultural recognition, performance is a practical tactic, and its relationship with the popular impacted the preservation of the Hampton House.

"Save the Hampton House!"

Pinkney was on the board of the Miami-Dade Heritage Trust when she contacted Louis Penelas, the brother of the city's mayor, Alex Penelas. She urged him to speak with his brother and get him to stop the demolition. Pinkney recalls him informing her that it was not so simple. A mayor could not use his power to stop a demolition when people had already been promised the job—it would be detrimental to his campaign. Instead, he advised Pinkney to have a press conference in front of the Hampton House. "Get some free food and advertise it as free. Get a band and get some music going. Get all the TV cameras you can to capture a large crowd saying 'save the Hampton House.'" When Pinkney told Penelas that she did not have the funds to pay for the food or the band, she recalls him saying, "Okay, I'll pay for the food and the band, but it's going to be Cuban food and a Cuban band." Pinkney succeeded in creating a theatrical moment of public popularity in favor of a site that had seemingly lost its cultural value. Media outlets were able to film a huge crowd championing the restoration of the Hampton House, and Mayor Penelas was in attendance. At the time, Pinkney was also contributing to the effort to save Miami Circle,[28] a sacred site built by the Tequesta people. Pinkney recalls Penelas stating that "if the city of Miami could spend 26 million to preserve the Circle, then we can spend some money to preserve Black history."[29] Pinkney had to choreograph communal popularity for political power.

The demolition was halted, but the state of Florida did not provide any money to Pinkney—even after the success of her resistive performance. She decided to apply for the general obligation bond, but as an assistant principal, she was unfamiliar with architectural and construction projects. She asked one of the leading historical preservationist architects in Miami, Richard Heisenbottle, for help with the application. She recalled him walking around the abandoned building filled with insects and drug needles in his "GQ suit," his Mercedes parked outside. He completed the entire application for free and signed it. Pinkney believes that this weighty signature inspired the county's approval of $4.6 million in restoration funds. However, the battle was not won. Pinkney said, "They fooled around so long, I don't think they really wanted to put money into this building." During a visit to the House in 2020, one of the preservationists informed me that he believed the county had been waiting for Pinkney to pass, banking on her request to be abandoned by the next generation. In 2006, the promised money finally came through, and a construction company accepted the bid, but they later rejected it because of the low project budget. By that time, Pinkney had a relationship with a commissioner in office, so she explained the situation to her before asking to increase the project funding to a little over $5 million. She got the money and a new company accepted, and then later rejected the project because it simply was not enough money to get the project done. Pinkney then sought out a third and final company that said they could get the project done for $6.1 million. The commissioner agreed to get the money but told Pinkney not to come back a third time. This new budget was enough to start the project.[30]

To date, the Historic Hampton House Restoration Project has not been completed. Due to the hotel being nearly destroyed, the majority of the building had to be reconstructed. Only a few structural elements could be preserved, such as the entryway stairs and the silver pillars in the now-repurposed event rental space. The team had to use archival pictures to design and reimagine the space. The staff has struggled to stage the house with historical artifacts from that time period, and this has required them to creatively choose what to display for visitors. They still house items that were disregarded during the Hampton House's period of abandonment, such as dishes, landlines, pieces of the old building, and unopened bottles of Coca-Cola. An entire wing of the Hampton House serves as an exhibition that performs a reenactment of a theatrical production of *One Night in Miami*. Miami New Drama donated the set from its 2018 production, and Pinkney says they were not in any position to refuse such an offer. This is a clear example of the dialogical relationship between popular performance and historic sites and how Black Miami structures can be more ephemeral than theatre.

The partially restored Hampton House has pictures of celebrities on its walls, and there is a noticeable imbalance of representations of women and the everyday people who knew the Hampton House as a community space. For example, one community member recalls taking swimming lessons at "the House" with other Black children, who were not widely welcomed at segregated swimming pools. Furthermore, during our interview, my grandmother asked Pinkney where all the money the local churches raised toward the restoration went, to which Pinkney replied that she never saw any of it. Their website reads:

> While Miami Beach was in the spotlight for its musicians and nightclub acts, it was Miami's Brownsville neighborhood and the Hampton House that the black performers returned to when the show was over. These musicians included Sammy Davis, Jr., Sam Cooke, Nat King Cole and many others. . . . Not only [Muhammad Ali], but other athletes also visited the Hampton House, including Jackie Robinson, Joe Louis, and Althea Gibson. It wasn't just a celebrity hangout, though. It was a hotspot for people of

the neighborhood on weekend evenings and after church on Sundays. . . . It was also the site for weekly meetings by the Congress for Racial Equality.

Dr. King [often visited] during the early '60s and delivered a version of his "I Have a Dream" speech at the Hampton House before his legendary oration at the March on Washington in 1963.[31]

This is a similar mythic, star-studded association that *One Night in Miami* orients toward, but it does not represent the performances of quotidian beauty found throughout Black Miami.

Much like the reconstruction of the Historic Hampton House, the set of the movie was a replica of the house built in Louisiana.[32] On a tour right after its release, I recall the Hampton House staff being excited about the film's potential to bring in more publicity. As they struggled to meet operational expenses and to finish the Hampton House, they contacted Amazon to talk about future collaborations. While Amazon did sponsor a film viewing in the space, the benefits stopped there.

The theatrical conjuring of Malcolm X, Cassius Clay, Sam Cooke, and Jim Brown illustrate how Black popularity can be used for legibility and mobility within white supremacist structures. However, these benefits are often unsustainable. Powers engages each character's dialogical positioning by staging confrontations of their individual and collective experiences of freedom that are tethered to the cultural capital and economic stature they access through the popular. Jim Brown's character voices a profound statement about professional Black athletes in the National Football League that resounds across time. He states, "We ain't nothin' but gladiators, Cash, and our ruler is still sittin' up there, in his box, givin' us the thumbs up or thumbs down."[33] In ancient Rome, gladiatorial battles were "a means of communicating the message of Imperial authority" that intensified as non-Roman peoples entered the empire.[34] With mangled fingers as evidence of corporeal sacrifice for success, Brown is made a popular culture legend from white spectatorship. At the top of the arena, the spectators with the highest degree of power safely enjoy the games, the boxing matches, and the battles.

To varying degrees, all four protagonists are put at risk due to their interactions with the popular. Their capital and power determine the relations of Black performers, and the distribution of these spectacles determines how they are viewed in the popular sphere. Powers presents that to be a Black man in the popular space is to face what Stuart Hall terms "relations of cultural power"[35] and to garner the suspicions of dominant and nondominant cultures. They are levied with the politics of racial uplift and entertainment in the face of violent white supremacy. In the play, Malcolm X becomes fixated on his camera because "photos never lie," and he is seemingly the only protagonist aware of the near impossibility of the right to privacy for Black men of their social standing. In addition to being monitored by Nation of Islam bodyguards that stand outside the room's door, X is doubly preoccupied with government surveillance of their conversation. Yet, there are no hotel records to confirm that this life-changing conversation took place. Although the play depicts preoccupations that the conversation could have been recorded, it remains an imagined act of ephemera. The history of Black popular culture can be a horizon for the present inheritors of the four men's legacy, and Black preservationists and creatives can form bridges to connect the differing temporalities. Although the four had enormous power and their economic mobility afforded them more opportunities during racial segregation, they were constantly expected to perform with their bodies while negotiating their Blackness.

Coda

On a tour of the Hampton House in August 2022, Edwin Sheppard, the Hampton House's branding ambassador, shared with me that the house had successfully acquired a historic landmark designation.[36] When he first contacted the officials, he explained to them that the Hampton House was the place where Malcolm X ran into Ali and where Martin Luther King rehearsed his famous "I Have a Dream" speech. After the house staff was informed that those facts would not earn them the designation alone, they were passed along a detailed application providing more information. Given that this arduous application packet took nearly a year to complete, the celebration Sheppard and the staff had when they found out the joyous news was well-earned. This recognition not only affords the Hampton House state recognition of its importance, but it also protects the site from being torn down or made unrecognizable. It cannot bring back its heyday, but it does grant structural protection as Miami's Black worlds continue to change.

Due to its elevation level, Brownsville is rumored to be the next battleground in the fight against environmental gentrification, a spatial practice that displaces low-income communities of color located on higher ground. By questioning the political capacity of theatre and performance in the struggle to prove Black Miami's historical value to the state, the popular urges an examination of the role of white supremacy in determining cultural value for marginalized groups. Although the Hampton House attracted a celebrity crowd and its starlit associations have been instrumental in securing interest in the site, it was also a place where the everyday people of Miami's Black communities could dress up and be seen in all their splendor. It was the memory of these times that spurred communal action in displays of popular cultural memory.

Performance theorist Harvey Young defines critical memory as "the act of reflecting upon and sharing recollections of black experience."[37] He states, "It looks back in time from a present-day perspective, and not only accounts for the evolution in culture, but also enables an imagining of what life would be like had things been different." In *Belonging: A Culture of Place*, bell hooks uses memory to urge us to "embrace an ethos of sustainability that is not solely about the appropriate care of the world's resources, but is also about the creation of meaning—the making of lives that we feel are worth living."[38] For Black Miami, sustainability can be historically restorative. Its history is intertwined with popular culture myths and celebrity speculations starring the "Magic City," and it is difficult not to question whether the loss of luminaries who once walked the Brownsville streets contributed to the Hampton House's abandonment. Appeals to the popular, theatremaking, and performance education have been crucial parts of the grassroots efforts to create meaning out of abandoned buildings and unpopular histories. Steadily regaining its shine, the Hampton House functions as a museum, event space, and communal arts education center. This work demonstrates the importance of embodiment when archives, monuments, and buildings fade with time; it proves that staging and historical reenactment can create both a past and a future.

Notes

1. Kemp Powers, *One Night in Miami* (London: Oberon Books, 2016).
2. Betty L. Simon, oral history interview, conducted by Mysia Anderson, Miami, 2022. The ID is her Civilian Registration Work Card.
3. Candacy Taylor, *Overground Railroad: The Green Book and the Roots of Black Travel in America* (New York: Abrams, 2020).
4. Stephen Best, *None Like Us: Blackness, Belonging, Aesthetic Life* (Durham, NC: Duke University Press, 2018).
5. N. D. B. Connolly, *A World More Concrete: Real Estate and the Remaking of Jim Crow* (Chicago: University of Chicago Press, 2014).
6. Connolly, *A World More Concrete*.
7. Candacy Taylor, *Overground Railroad: The Green Book and the Roots of Black Travel in America* (New York: Abrams, 2020).
8. Taylor, *Overground Railroad*.
9. Taylor, *Overground Railroad*.
10. Jonathan Scott Holloway, *Jim Crow Wisdom: Memory and Identity in Black America Since 1940* (Chapel Hill: University of North Carolina Press, 2013).
11. Holloway, *Jim Crow Wisdom*.
12. Stuart Hall, "What Is This 'Black' in Black Popular Culture?" *Social Justice/Global Options* 20, no. 1/2 (51–52) (Spring-Summer 1993): 104–14.

13. Donnette Francis and Allison Harris, "Introduction: Looking for Black Miami," *Anthurium: A Caribbean Studies Journal* 16, no. 1 (2020).

14. Jesse M. Keenan, Thomas Hill, and Anurag Gumber, "Climate Gentrification: From Theory to Empiricism in Miami-Dade County, Florida," *Environmental Research Letters* 13, no. 5, April 23, 2018 (Bristol, UK: IOP Publishing).

15. Enid C. Pinkney, oral history interview, conducted by Mysia Anderson at Hampton House, Miami, 2022.

16. Pickney, oral history interview.

17. Pickney, oral history interview.

18. Pickney, oral history interview.

19. Pickney, oral history interview.

20. Pickney, oral history interview.

21. Pickney, oral history interview.

22. Loren King, "Screenwriter Kemp Powers on Finding Truth and Beauty in 'One Night in Miami,'" Motion Picture Association (website), February 2, 2021, accessed June 5, 2023.

23. Saidiya Hartman, "Venus in Two Acts," *Small Axe* 12, no. 2.

24. Pickney, oral history interview.

25. Diana Taylor, *The Archive and the Repertoire: Performing Cultural Memory in the Americas* (Durham, NC: Duke University Press, 2007).

26. Pickney, oral history interview.

27. Taylor, *Archive and the Repertoire.*

28. Miami Circle National Historic Landmark, Trail of Florida's Indian Heritage, March 28, 2022, accessed April 22, 2022.

29. Pickney, oral history interview.

30. Pickney, oral history interview.

31. "History." Historic Hampton House Museum and Cultural Center (website), accessed May 29, 2022.

32. Loren King, "Screenwriter Kemp Powers on Finding Truth and Beauty in 'One Night in Miami.'"

33. Powers, *One Night in Miami.*

34. Alison Futrell, *Blood in the Arena* (Austin: University of Texas Press. 1997).

35. Stuart Hall, "What Is This 'Black' in Black Popular Culture?"

36. Edwin Sheppard, tour and interview, Hampton House, Miami, 2022.

37. Harvey Young, *Embodying Black Experience: Stillness, Critical Memory, and the Black Body* (Ann Arbor: University of Michigan Press, 2010).

38. bell hooks, *Belonging: A Culture of Place* (New York: Routledge, 1990).

The Popularity of Contemporary Singaporean Pantomime

Chelsea Curto

CONTEMPORARY PANTOMIME (OR "panto," as it is colloquially known) refers to a nostalgia-inducing, interactive musical fairy tale performed by gender-bending actors.[1] Scholars repeatedly emphasize that pantomime is the most popular form of theatre in Europe.[2] The global popularity of pantomime stems from and primarily abides in the United Kingdom, but pantomime scholar Simon Sladen has expressed interest in the ways pantomime manifests overseas.[3] Many former British colonies have an ongoing relationship with the popular art form. Pantomime began in the Victorian era, when "every aspect of popular culture contrived to instill pride in the British imperial achievement."[4] However, scholarly interest has stopped short of explicitly analyzing the ways in which contemporary pantomime functions differently in postcolonial societies than in Great Britain.

The country of Singapore was founded on British principles but has evolved to reflect sociopolitical concerns unique to its culture.[5] While British pantomime was performed in Singapore by British subjects throughout its history as a British colony, contemporary pantomime emerged in Singapore when Ivan Heng founded local theatre company Wild Rice in 2000 and began staging pantomimes three years later.[6] In the two decades since, Wild Rice has produced an annual pantomime almost every year. In 2017, I had the pleasure of watching a production of the original pantomime *Mama White Snake*, written by celebrated Singaporean playwright Alfian Sa'at. The production was recognizably panto: There was interactive theatricality, men dressed as women, musical comedy, and a hero's journey. But the experience of sitting in Singapore's Drama Centre Theatre felt different from watching *Dick Whittington* at the Lyric Hammersmith in London. The plot was drawn from a Chinese folktale instead of a Victorian classic. The characters spoke Singlish instead of Cockney-accented English. The references were hyperlocal. The performers were familiar faces and as they built rapport with the audience, I felt proud to be a resident of Singapore who had grown up in the culture. I felt part of a recognizable community.

In contrast to British pantomime, which is based on a long-standing, self-referential tradition, theatre artists in Singapore use the popular form of pantomime to express a shared, multicultural national identity. This essay uses examples from Wild Rice pantomimes to document the uniquely Singaporean components of contemporary Singaporean pantomime and analyze how theatre artists in Singapore use the popular form of pantomime to articulate the language, culture, and politics of postcolonial Singapore society. Hopefully, this work will inspire future researchers to conduct similar analyses of other postcolonial pantomime traditions and contribute to the breadth of knowledge about how this popular theatre genre has evolved beyond the British tradition that produced it.

Singaporean pantomime is a different entity from British pantomime. Its conventions may draw on British standards, but Singaporeans have coopted the low art form and made it their own. Recognizable elements in the work of Singaporean panto playwrights remain similar to the British pantomime genre. Gender-bending is common throughout the cast, the plot is based on a beloved classic fairy tale and follows a quest story arc, the dialogue with the audience is interactive, and the productions contain upbeat music and side-splitting comedy.[7] However, a "by Singaporeans, for Singaporeans" mentality proves a clear distinction between British and Singaporean pantomime. There are three specific structures that are common in contemporary pantomime from each country, but function differently in Singapore than in Great Britain: the role of the Dame, the interactivity between pantomime performers and the audience, and topically referential jokes. British pantomime may have established these structures as inherent to pantomime, but Singaporean pantomime has adapted them in ways that articulate and reify postcolonial national identity.

Singaporean pantomime deviates significantly from British pantomime in the way it treats the character of the Dame. The character of the Dame is such a highly recognizable figure of British pantomime that most scholars accept her appearance as a foregone conclusion. Millie Taylor identifies the Dame as "the principal driver of the pantomime . . . played by a man dressed as a woman but not in drag."[8] Taylor further theorizes that "the dame connects with the audience on two levels: as a mother figure talking about family problems and social issues; as a man pretending to be a woman to an audience who sees through the pretence [sic] and shares the joke."[9] In the tradition of commedia dell'arte (from which pantomime traces its roots), the art of playing the Dame is passed down from master to apprentice.[10] Dames reach celebrity status; in her analysis of branding in contemporary pantomime, Martina Lipton identifies that Dames Berwick Kaler and Kenneth Alan Taylor are household names in Great Britain.[11]

The Dame in Singaporean pantomime is not the recognizable force it is in British pantomime. Perhaps subconsciously, Singaporean pantomime artists have challenged and subverted the traditional Dame character because they are articulating a new, postcolonial identity that does not rely on the double figure of mother and cross-dressing man. Some Singaporean pantomimes feature characters that seem like they could be Dames, but closer inspection reveals that the Singaporean version of the pantomime has transformed the Dame role. At first glance, Cinderella's fairy godmother as Fairy God Makcik (the word "makcik" is Malay for Auntie), played by a male actor, seems like a Dame character.[12] However, Fairy God Makcik does not open the show, he does not set the audience's expectations for interaction, and the actor who played the role in *Cinderel-LAH* (Najip Ali) was not the highest-status performer in the piece, as is generally the case with the Dame in British panto.[13]

Singaporean pantomime tends to de-emphasize the Dame figure or remove it altogether. Wild Rice has produced two different versions of *Aladdin*, the first in 2004 and the second in 2011. In the traditional British pantomime, the Dame role in *Aladdin* is Widow Twankey. While both Wild Rice productions featured an actor in an analogous role (Widow Wong Kee, Aladdin's mother), the star power of both productions was centered around the actors playing Aladdin (film actor Robin Goh in 2004 and Asian Idol Winner Hady Mirza in 2011), and the comedic and audience-interaction function usually performed by the Dame was primarily filled by the Wizard. In his Singaporean version of *Jack and the Beanstalk*, playwright Joel Tan omits the traditional Dame entirely. Jack's mother is played by a female actor and the comedic cross-dressing is done by two additional narrators in the story, Kopi Gao and Siew Dai.

Singaporean pantomime artists seem to suggest that two Dames are sometimes better than one. Kopi Gao and Siew Dai of *Jack and the Bean-Sprout* are one example of double Dame characters, but we see similar duet Dame-ing happen in *Mama White Snake* with the characters of Auntie Green and Mama White, as well as in *Beauty and the Beast* with Beauty's two ugly and shallow stepsisters, Brandy and Desiree.[14] Wild Rice's 2022 production of *The Amazing Celestial Race* featured two narrators, B1 and B2, but neither can be considered Dames, as the actors who played them did not play against gender and played many other roles as well.[15] While a male actor playing a female character for laughs is a common sight in both Singaporean and British pantomime, the recognizable role of a single famous and practiced comedic Dame who serves a particular narrative function is not evident in Singaporean pantomime. Instead, the narrative function of the Dame is decentralized and shared among the cast. It is not a single character that guides an audience through the pantomime story but the ensemble. Taking the most recognizable role in British pantomime, the Dame, and subverting it metonymizes the postcolonial relationship between Singapore and Great Britain.

The Dame is not the only role in British pantomime that Singaporean pantomime transforms. British pantomime features extensive interactivity between performers and the audience. Millie Taylor specifies that while all members of the pantomime company may interact directly with the audience, two panto characters in particular carry the brunt of the audience interaction requirement. Taylor says it is typically the job of the young comic to set the expectation that an audience will "respond vocally when required" by building a relationship with the children in the audience, and it falls on the Dame to connect with the adults in the audience.[16] Taylor theorizes that the many opportunities for audience participation in pantomime serve to "encourage the audience to act as a body and therefore to take part in a communal experience, to become a community for the time and place of performance."[17] Singaporean pantomime, in contrast to British pantomime, offers fewer opportunities for audience participation. In British pantomime, the direct address at the opening teaches children in the audience how to be a pantomime audience member and guides the audience toward a shared, communal experience within the walls of the theatre. In Singaporean pantomimes, the direct address at the opening serves to build rapport with the audience as a whole—adult and child alike—and casts them in the role of Singaporean, both inside and outside the walls of the theatre. In this way, Singaporean pantomime uses the interaction between company and audience to construct and reinforce identity.

A major way Singaporean pantomime casts the audience in the role of Singaporean is by using the amalgamated local language to build rapport and create a shared identity. Singaporean pantomime is the only English-language theatre genre in Singapore written primarily and unapologetically in Singlish. Singlish is an English-based language with shortened sentence structure and vocabulary drawn from Malay, Tamil, and multiple Chinese dialects. Singlish is rarely used in formal contexts, such as on the stage. The Speak Good English Movement of the early 2000s sought to decrease the usage of "poor" English, which is the hallmark of local speech.[18] Mediacorp, Singapore's state-run media agency, declines to produce content that features anything but Standard English (or Malay, Tamil, or Mandarin Chinese).[19] As a result, while the population at large speaks Singlish daily, the metalanguage is rarely used in formal contexts except as a form of humor.

Contrary to its disuse in formal settings, Singaporean pantomime embraces the linguistic patterns of Singlish. By conversing directly with the pantomime audience using local speech, pantomime artists create a community like the one Taylor ascribes to British audiences but that extends beyond the theatre. Consider the opening scene of the 2013 rehearsal script of *Jack and the Bean-Sprout*:

> Kopi Gao: Eh, Hello! My name is Kopi Gao!
> Siew Dai: And I am Siew Dai!
> Kopi Gao: We work here at Hougang Block 415 there

> sell drinks. Our shop hor, we make the best KOPI GAO!
> Siew Dai: SIEW DAI!
> Together: KOPI GAO SIEW DAI![20]
> Kopi Gao: Eh you all don't drink Kopitiam one right, you all is drink Starbucks one hor?
> Siew Dai: Hannorh! Spoil market until now our kopitiam also must upgrade! Eh ask you, how many of you here live in Hougang? Show show! Your lift also never upgrade, that's why so fit. Wah not a lot ah, you all I think is live condo one lah! Only rich kids can come see show hor![21]

The characters Kopi Gao and Siew Dai do not ask for vocal participation—simply a show of hands—and the question they ask is personal: Where do you live?[22] In the same breath, the aunties make fun of the audience for having money. In British pantomime, if a character asks the audience a question, it will be pantomime related—as Taylor states, "audience participation . . . provid[es] a bridge between the worlds of the story, 'pantoland' and the real world of the audience."[23] In Singaporean pantomime, the characters ask the audience to identify who they are as a community outside of pantoland. The use of Singlish reinforces the Singaporean identity the characters model.

The characters of Kopi Gao and Siew Dai also play into the linguistic class division around Singlish that a Singapore resident audience will immediately recognize. The two characters are kopitiam aunties, older women who work at a kopitiam, a drinks stall that sells local coffee (kopi in Malay). Local Singaporeans will invariably frequent these stalls daily, but there is an inherent and complex divide. Hawker center workers are respected cultural icons that nobody in class-conscious Singapore wants to become. The characters are immediately recognizable caricatures of a beloved institution and position themselves in opposition to globalized, gentrified, non-Singaporean Starbucks baristas.

Jack and the Bean-Sprout is not the only Singaporean pantomime to utilize Singlish to build audience rapport and articulate national identity. The title of the Singaporean pantomime *Cinderel-LAH* is an obvious reference to the Singlish suffix. The characters use Singlish expressions throughout the text.[24] In the Singaporean pantomime *Mama White Snake*, the two characters Auntie Green and Mama White repeat a bit where Mama White cannot pronounce the Chinese phrase ma fan, meaning troublesome, with the proper tones—despite being dressed in full Chinese opera costume and played by a Chinese-Singaporean actor.[25] Not only does this comedic bit reinforce the multilingualism of Singapore society, but it also serves to build rapport with a universal experience. Struggling with Chinese tones is something everyone in Singapore has either witnessed or experienced.

While British pantomime focuses on constructing a shared experience within the theatre through audience interaction, Singaporean pantomime features a more confrontational approach to audience interaction that serves as a critique from within that catalyzes the interrogative process of the construction of identity. Wealth inequality in Singapore is something most are aware of but never speak about. At the start of *Jack and the Bean-Sprout*, Kopi Gao and Siew Dai explicitly poke fun at the audience for being wealthy, but that is not the only place where a satirical criticism of wealth inequality occurs. In act 2, Jack and his mother have used their windfall to move out of Hougang and into a fancy condo in Buangkok, a neighboring district. The condo is called Le Buang in reference to the Singaporean predilection for making *atas* (expensive or fancy) places sound vaguely European by adding "la" or "le" before the name.[26] In a song called "Le Buang," the chorus sings about the property, "Like schools nearby, swimming pools the size of income divides / . . . Such quality inequality is the taste of success!" The target audience of Wild Rice's pantomimes, as Kopi Gao and Siew Dai explicitly point out in the opening sequence, tends to be in a higher income bracket. They are more likely to live in condominiums like the fictional "Le Buang" than in the heartland apartments of Hougang. Pantomime explicitly tackles issues that are either hinted at or completely ignored in more mainstream, so-called legitimate theatre and encourages a Singaporean audience to recognize themselves.

Singaporean pantomime uses the satirical strategy of critique from within to articulate national identity. Another example from *Jack and the Bean-Sprout* that engages its audience in confrontational, critical dialogue is when the play indirectly calls out Singaporeans for being xenophobic. Once again, the pantomime audience is the butt of the joke. When Jack climbs the bean sprout, he meets a cerulean alien named Xeno, who laments that the giant utilizes her talents to serve him, but nobody talks to her because her skin is blue. This is certainly a veiled reference to the tendency of wealthy Singaporeans to hire foreign domestic workers. The relatively wealthy pantomime audience is obviously the target of criticism. Why do they put up with this abuse? I propose it is because the audience interactivity of Singaporean pantomime explicitly addresses sensitive topics in a matter-of-fact way. It is uncomfortable to be called out for complicity in xenophobia and wealth inequality, but as self-aware Singaporeans, the pantomime audience knows that the criticism is well-deserved. The fact that theatremakers who are Singaporean themselves create this satire makes the social critique more palatable and facilitates the process of identity construction.

In addition to the structure of audience interaction, the humor in Singaporean pantomime serves to create a sense of national identity within the audience watching. A recurring joke in the text of *Jack and the Bean-Sprout* comes in the form of two civil servants. They appear first as *gahmen* (government) workers from the Housing Development Board. Later in the play, they appear as civil servants from the Inland Revenue Authority and bind the main characters up in literal red tape. Finally, at the end of the play, we see the same two characters in fatigues and learn that they are in the military. When asked about it, one says, "We did such a good job as tax collectors, they transferred us to the army, this is called civil service rotation!"[27] The joke is not libelous because it is simply a fact—the Singaporean government is notorious for shuffling assignments. A resident Singaporean audience sees their reality in the satire onstage. The jokes are not actually critical of the government. They ask Singaporeans to articulate who they are as a nation.

The opening scene of *Jack and the Bean-Sprout* contains one of these seemingly political jokes that illustrates how Singaporean pantomime challenges existing hegemony as a strategy for engaging in the articulation of identity. Not only is Hougang a heartland community, but it is also one of the only districts in Singapore that the People's Action Party (PAP) does not govern.[28] At the time of Tan's writing in 2013, Hougang was governed by the opposition Worker's Party, the symbol of which is a blue hammer (as opposed to the PAP's red lightning bolt). Siew Dai's reference to the lifts (elevators) not working in Hougang is political. Because the opposition, which has less political power, governs the district, it is common for citizens to complain that their amenities are not as well-kept as those of their peers in PAP-governed areas. The majority party PAP encourages this perception. If things do not go well in opposition areas, perhaps the citizens will reinstate the majority party at the next election. After Kopi Gao and Siew Dai and the audience call in the Principal Boy of the story (played by a male performer in the 2013 production in contrast to British pantomime custom, where the Principal Boy is nearly always played by a female performer), Jack, they burst into a song called "Hougang," the lyrics of which go in part:

> And over here's the kopitiam where everybody meets
> Our MP got no office so he meets us where he eats!
> My mother says Hougang is an Opposition Land!
> Who needs lightning, we got hammer in our hand![29]

The references to the symbols of the dueling parties are obvious. The second line of the excerpt refers to the fact that historically, opposition leaders were hindered from obtaining office space.[30] In fact, it was not until the most recent elections in 2020 that Pritam Singh, Leader of the Opposition, was afforded office space in the Parliament Building.[31] The political reference in the playscript seems subversive until one considers that the playwright offers no political opinion here, only facts. As Terence Chong repeatedly states in

The Theatre and the State in Singapore, the relationship between theatres and the government is symbiotic.[32] Wild Rice receives significant support from the state-funded Singapore National Arts Council (NAC), and the Singapore government does not want to appear to censor arts organizations. That is not to say that the government cannot or will not censor theatre companies—Chong's book includes 108 separate index entries relating to the topic of censorship, and his text is only 171 pages long. Singapore's censors are notoriously fickle and difficult to please.[33] However, while pantomimes such as *Jack and the Bean-Sprout* appear at first glance to be subversively political, closer inspection reveals that the criticism has no bite. Instead, the jokes are shared by performers with an audience who sees the truth in them.

Pantomimes like *Jack and the Bean-Sprout* hold up a mirror to the populace, highlighting inconsistencies within the national sense of identity depicted on the pantomime stage and challenging audience members to question what they see. Singapore is a multiracial society. Racial harmony is legislated, and everything from government housing to hiring practices is subject to strict guidelines designed to keep the racial balance fair and equitable. In 2010, the United Nations sent a Special Rapporteur to Singapore to interrogate the polity's approach to race-related issues. When the UN released a special report of its findings, which unequivocally identified blind spots within Singapore's systems and policies that result in racial and other discrimination, the PAP-dominated Singapore Ministry of Foreign Affairs took issue with nearly every conclusion in the report.[34] In *Jack and the Bean-Sprout*, Joel Tan uses exaggeration and farce to emphasize the UN's findings and criticize the PAP's official position on racial construction and performativity.

Jack and the Bean-Sprout includes a transgressive scene where the leader of the KauKauKau, Tua Hia, reveals that he has changed his race to subvert the strict punishment awarded to him for engaging in loan shark activities. When Widow Neo sees Tua Hia, she does not recognize him. He tells her:

> Tua Hia: I escaped Changi Prison through the toilet,
> Widow Neo, then I went to the KauKauKau plastic surgeon and they changed my face, changed my skin and even burnt off my finger prints.
> Widow Neo: Does that mean . . .
> Tua Hia: Yes! I was Tan Tua Hia but now I am Tua Hia Bin Tua Hia. And I LOVE it. Being Melayu is more fun: life is bigger, got bigger appetite, got bigger families, bigger eyes, bigger chance of winning Singapore idol, bigger everything! And when I go Malaysia, they don't try to cheat my money.[35]

There are many racialized assumptions at play in this exchange. Tua Hia states that being Malay is more fun and highlights the positive stereotypes associated with the second-largest racial group in Singapore: a good singing voice and rounder eyes. However, this sort of tokenism cheapens the rich cultural differences that exist between the racial groups in Singapore. It also undermines the valid critique that things are not quite as rosy as the PAP would have citizens believe. Despite legislated racial harmony, Singaporeans of racial minorities report facing severe bias, and scholars declaim Singapore's policies as counterproductive.[36] By presenting race as a farcical social construct, playwright Joel Tan highlights the stereotypes and inequities currently faced by Singaporeans in local society. By staging the pantomime, Wild Rice requires an audience to see themselves in the hypocrisy and grapple with what it means to be Singaporean.

It might seem as though Singaporean pantomime creates a sense of postcolonial national identity solely through critical or adversarial means. However, Singaporean pantomime also fosters connection with an audience through topical references that generate joy. Whether one is Singaporean or a resident of Singapore, food culture is central to Singapore society. Proving the adage that the way to the heart is through the stomach, cultural references to the country's favorite pastime—eating—abound. The Fairy God Makcik in *Cinderel-LAH* first appears as a hawker auntie selling kueh, and later nasi lemak.[37] In *Peter Pan in Serangoon Gardens*, Michael explains the Singaporean obsession with food delivery services.[38] In *Mama White Snake*, Principal Boy Meng, played by a male actor, is tested by Mama White and Auntie Green on which foods are warming and which are cooling.[39] But the best examples of how Singaporean pantomime uses food references to build rapport and construct identity with a Singaporean audience are found in *Jack and the Bean-Sprout*.

In *Jack and the Bean-Sprout*, the titular Singaporean riff on the traditional beanstalk is directly referenced in the text by the Chinese name for the popular beansprout vegetable: tougay. When Jack takes his pet, Ah Kow, to Tekka Market to pay off his mother's gambling debt, he is tricked by a pair of low-lifes (naturally named after food—Orh Luat and Orh Nee, oyster omelet and yam paste, respectively) into trading Ah Kow for a bag of beans that grow into a giant bean sprout ("Widow Neo: It's a giant tougeh [*sic*]! They were magic beans!").[40] At the end of act 2, Jack escapes from the giant down the bean sprout. We hear the giant exclaim, "FEE FI FO FUM! I'll stuff your head into a bun!"[41] The army men shoot down the bean sprout, and we think the giant is killed until the very end of the play when it is revealed that not only has the giant survived, but he just wanted to taste the amazing food in Singapore—he says, "FEE FI FO FUM! Singapore food is why I come! . . . NASI PADANG CHEE CHEONG FUN. AYAM PENYET SA POH FUN."[42] The rhyme is a series of celebrated Singapore dishes. Nasi padang is a Malay term for steamed rice served with a variety of different dishes, chee cheong fun is a type of Cantonese dim sum rice noodle dish, ayam penyet is a Javanese fried chicken dish, and sa poh fun (more typically anglicized sar po fan) is Chinese clay-pot chicken. Much like the melting pot of Singapore culture, food bridges the gap between disparate characters and serves as a culminating plot point in the pantomime.

Singaporean pantomime may have evolved from the traditions set by its British predecessors, but the popular art form functions differently in Singapore than it does in the UK, and the pantomimes themselves reflect these differences. From the character of the Dame to the interaction with the audience, from the political jokes to the mild rebukes, from the language used to the references to food, Singaporean pantomime requires an audience to articulate who they are as a nation. Singaporean pantomime is a popular form of theatre that differs significantly from its British ancestor, and these differences serve to reify identity in postcolonial Singaporean society.

Notes

1. This definition of pantomime is an amalgamation of scholarship on the subject. Refer to Robert Marsden's article "Pantomime," in the *Routledge Companion to Audiences and the Performing Arts* (New York: Routledge, 2022) and Jude Christian's "It's Behind You! Oh No, It Isn't: The Joys and Challenges of Making Contemporary Pantomime," *Times Literary Supplement*, no. 6090–6091 (December 20, 2019).

2. Millie Taylor, *British Pantomime Performance* (Bristol, UK: Intellect, 2007), 73.

3. Simon Sladen created and maintains the only extent database devoted to pantomime, the National Database of Pantomime Performance. For further reading of Sladen's comments on the global reach of pantomime, see "The Globality of Pantomime: A Brief Excursion," *Popular Entertainment Studies* 3, no. 2: 65–71, and "How the Globe Warmed to Pantomime," *Stage*, November 27, 2014.

4. Jeffrey Richards, *The Golden Age of Pantomime* (New York: I. B. Taurus, 2015), 20.

5. Sharon Siddique and Chan Heng Chee, *Singapore's Multiculturalism: Evolving Diversity* (London: Routledge, 2019).

6. Examples of colonial pantomime in Singapore abound. As early as 1856, *Straits Times*, Singapore's newspaper, advertised comic pantomimes imported from overseas that were to be performed locally (Anon., "Page 4 Advertisements Column 1" *Straits Times*. [Singapore], January 1, 1856). In 1930, a Mrs. Clarke produced the pantomime *Sleeping Beauty* in aid of the

SPCA; in 1949, a radio play version of the pantomime *Aladdin* was produced (Anon., "Malacca 'Panto,'" *The Singapore Free Press and Mercantile Advertiser* [Singapore], December 10, 1930, and Anon., "'Panto' Again" *Straits Times* [Singapore], January 10, 1949). Conspicuously, it appears that most English-language theatre and all pantomime were produced and executed by British performers for largely expatriate or military audiences. In 1980, a review in Singapore's *New Nation* newspaper gives insight into a pantomime produced by Singapore's oldest theatre company, The Stage Club, which is still active today. Suzanne Stokes wrote a version of *Cinderella* that combined the characters of the beloved children's story with Miss Piggy and Wonder Woman, ostensibly written (as were her past opuses *Aladdin* and *Sleeping Beauty*) "for local audiences"—however, the only explicit reference in the performance review to anything that can be construed as remotely postcolonial Singaporean is the intracultural substitution of the stinky Southeast Asian durian fruit for Cinderella's traditional pumpkin. See Anon., "Wonder Woman and Miss Piggy in Cinderella" *New Nation* [Singapore], January 5, 1981. In logos and other decorative contexts, the name of the theatre company is sometimes styled with an exclamation point in place of the I in "wild" (W!ld Rice). The company itself uses a conventional letter I in promotional text about their own history and productions, so we have followed that model.

7. For a sustained discussion of the elements inherent to British pantomime, refer to Millie Taylor's *British Pantomime Performance* (Bristol, UK: Intellect Books, 2007). A more populist analysis of the repertoire and performers in British pantomime is Maureen Hughes's *A History of Pantomime* (Barnsley, UK: Pen and Sword, 2014), which declares pantomime "essentially a British thing" and celebrates "how wonderful [it is] to have a style that belongs to just the British" (12). Any discussion of British pantomime should also include a reference to the elder bible of the art form, *Oh Yes It Is! A History of Pantomime* by Gerald Frow (London: British Broadcasting Corporation, 1985).

8. Taylor, *British Pantomime Performance*, 14.

9. Taylor, *British Pantomime Performance*, 106–7.

10. Simon Sladen, "From Mother Goose to Master: Training Networks and Knowledge Transfer in Contemporary British Pantomime," *Theatre, Dance and Performance Training* 8, no. 2 (May 4, 2017): 206.

11. Martina Lipton, "Celebrity versus Tradition: 'Branding' in Modern British Pantomime," *New Theatre Quarterly* 23, no. 2 (2007): 142.

12. Selena Tan, *Cinderel-LAH [Rehearsal]* (Singapore: Wild Rice, 2010), 52.

13. That distinction would certainly have gone to Gurmit Singh, celebrated star of local Singapore television show *Phua Chu Kang Pte Ltd*, who played the character Ali in *Cinderel-LAH* (an analog of the Buttons character in British *Cinderella* pantomime). See Taylor, *British Pantomime Performance*, 41.

14. *Jack and the Bean-Sprout*: "About Us: Past Productions: 2013," Wild Rice theatre company (website), Singapore; *Mama White Snake*: "About Us: Past Productions: 2017," Wild Rice theatre company (website), Singapore; *Beauty and the Beast*: "About Us: Past Productions: 2009," Wild Rice theatre company (website), Singapore, accessed May 17, 2023.

15. The Amazing Celestial Race: "About Us: Past Productions: 2022," Wild Rice theatre company (website), Singapore, accessed May 17, 2023.

16. Taylor, *British Pantomime Performance*, 124.

17. Taylor, *British Pantomime Performance*, 2007, 132. For examples of the many ways audiences are encouraged to participate in British pantomime, see chapter 8 of Taylor's text.

18. Lionel Wee, "'Burdens' and 'Handicaps' in Singapore's Language Policy: On the Limits of Language Management," *Language Policy* 9, no. 2 (2019): 99.

19. Republic of Singapore, Infocomm Media Development Authority (IMDA), *Content Code for Nationwide Managed Transmission Linear Television Services*, 2019: 8.3.

20. Kopi is typically made by brewing a very strong, thick (*gao*) coffee base that is then diluted with water and sweetened condensed milk when the aunty fills a drink order. Siew dai is Hokkien for "less sweet." The aunties' chant of "KOPI GAO SIEW DAI" is a play on words—it is both their names and the popular drink order that they sell at their stall.

21. Joel Tan, *Jack and the Bean-Sprout* (rehearsal) (Singapore: Wild Rice, 2013), 2. Siew Dai's last line in the excerpt can be translated as "Enough! Your expectations are so high, now we must upgrade our coffee shop! Hey, I ask you, how many of you in the audience live in Hougang? Raise your hands! Your elevators don't get serviced regularly by the government, that's why you are in such good shape. Oh wow, not many of you live in Hougang, I think you all must live in private housing! Makes sense, only rich people can afford to buy tickets to this play."

22. Hougang is a heartland neighborhood in Singapore—a residential area where locals live in government-subsidized Housing Development Board (HDB) flats. Government-subsidized housing in Singapore does not have a negative connotation. Most Singaporeans live in HDB flats.

23. Taylor, *British Pantomime Performance*, 123.

24. Selena Tan, *Cinderel-LAH* (rehearsal) (Singapore: Wild Rice, 2011).

25. Alfian Sa'at, *Mama White Snake* (rehearsal) (Singapore: Wild Rice, 2017), 4–5.

26. In the Paya Lebar area of Singapore, there is a condominium called Le Crescendo, and at the time of publication, Le Quest is one of the newest property developments in Singapore.

27. Tan, *Jack and the Bean-Sprout* (rehearsal), 57.

28. The People's Action Party (PAP) is the political party that has been in control of Singapore since the polity was founded in 1965. See Hussin Mutalib, *Parties and Politics: A Study of Opposition Parties and the PAP in Singapore*.

29. Tan, *Jack and the Bean-Sprout* (rehearsal), 4. Jack is designated Jack (Neo) in the script, one of many references to Singapore's homegrown movie star of the same name.

30. Department of State, Committee on Foreign Affairs, *Country Reports on Human Rights Practices for 1993* (Washington, DC: Government Printing Office, 1994).

31. Rei Kurohi, "Parliament Sets Out Duties and Privileges of Leader of the Opposition Pritam Singh," *Straits Times*, July 20, 2021.

32. Terence Chong, *The Theatre and the State in Singapore* (New York: Routledge, 2013), 170.

33. Terence Chong, "'Back Regions' and 'Dark Secrets' in Singapore: The Politics of Censorship and Liberalisation," *Space and Polity* 14, no. 3 (2010): 235.

34. James Gomez, "Politics and Ethnicity: Framing Racial Discrimination in Singapore," Third International Conference on International Studies (2010): 6.

35. Tan, *Jack and the Bean-Sprout* (rehearsal), 17. Tan Hua Hia is a Chinese name; the surname is first and the given name last. Tan Hua bin Tan Hua is (sort of) a Malay name—the surname is the father's name, placed after the word *bin* for men or *binte* for women.

36. Selvaraj Velayutham, "Everyday Racism in Singapore," in *Multiculturalism*, ed. Amanda Wise and Selvaraj Velayutham (New York: Palgrave Macmillan, 2009), 257.

37. Kueh is a sweet rice-based dessert cake and nasi lemak is a coconut rice dish with fish or chicken.

38. Thomas Lim, *Peter Pan in Serangoon Gardens* (Rehearsal) (Singapore: Wild Rice, 2019), 54.

39. Alfian Sa'at, *Mama White Snake* (Rehearsal) (Singapore: Wild Rice, 2017), 9. Warming and cooling foods are a Traditional Chinese Medicine (TCM) phenomenon.

40. Tan, *Jack and the Bean-Sprout* (Rehearsal), 34.

41. Tan, *Jack and the Bean-Sprout* (Rehearsal), 58.

42. Tan, *Jack and the Bean-Sprout* (Rehearsal), 62.

Promoting a Popular Body

The Stage, Couture, and the Creation of the Female Form in the Late Nineteenth and Early Twentieth Centuries

Sarah McCarroll

IN 1875, JEAN-PHILLIPE Worth joined his father, the Parisian couturier Charles Frederick Worth, as the presumptive artistic heir of the family's renowned fashion house.[1] For his first assignment, the younger Worth found himself designing thirty costumes for an American tour by actress Genevieve Ward.[2] Worth gowns were already famous by this time, and the willingness of the House of Worth and other major fashion houses of the era to dress actresses, in addition to women who moved in high society, meant that these ensembles became available to public view when they were used as costumes in plays set in the contemporary social world. Couture gowns worn onstage and off were also regularly reproduced in the popular illustrated press, which expanded the audience reached by couture design. In these periodicals, Worth gowns were worn by the famous women of the day, including stage performers like Ward. And the styles of dresses that were available to view onstage or purchase from Worth's ateliers changed with increasing frequency between the 1860s and World War I as the cycles of seasonal fashion that we recognize today developed.

Viewing couture-gowned actresses, both onstage and in the press, popularized fashions and helped to create and spread visual paradigms of a popular body. In this essay, I argue that the advent of a popular figure was an integral part of the development of fashion in the late-nineteenth century. This popular body was disseminated via popular society stages of the day on the Continent, in England, and in America by actresses who wore couture gowns onstage and who were described and pictured in the press.

Here I seek to explore the ecology by which a particular body shape becomes "in" for a time period. I argue that fashion designers took advantage of the late-nineteenth-century stage's reliance on visual realism to cultivate a space in which their work could be advertised on a body that advantageously showed it to a wider public than would ever set foot inside a couture showroom. Just as fashion developed during the period as one element of the ever-more-elaborate rituals of wealthy culture, the relationship of designers to the stage and performers evolved as an important component in an increasingly complex system of images that promulgated a popular, fashionable body. To examine this ecology of bodies, the stage, the press, designers, garments, and fashion ephemera, I position artifacts of material culture, including clothing, fashion illustrations, and sewing patterns, as an archive of popularity. They serve as a record of what was fashionable, desirable, and therefore marketable.[3] This essay explores the development of fashion and its relationship to the stage, often turning to the paradigm-setting House of Worth and the theatrical design work of the couturiere Lucile as exemplars of the dynamics through which fashion worn onstage worked to circulate ideas of the popular body.

Charles Frederick Worth is regularly credited as being the first fashion designer in the modern sense of the term. Worth was an Englishman who moved to Paris to pursue a career in the garment industry; he initially worked for Gagelin, a firm that sold textiles and ready-made garments.[4] In 1858, Worth opened his own firm and his work soon came to the attention of the Empress Eugénie. Second Empire France, under Napoleon III and Eugénie, saw a resurgence of court culture and style that had been absent since the French Revolution. At the same time, the post–Industrial Revolution dispersion of wealth beyond the aristocracy created an imperative for increased complexity in fashionable life as a way of culturally means-testing those who tried to break into the upper-class world.[5] These unspoken cultural tests helped create the series of fashion "seasons" that are still in use today. Fashion had to change regularly to provide new styles for those who served as consumers of and gatekeepers to the fashionable world of high society; the ability to afford a refreshed wardrobe every three to six months was one way of ensuring suitability for acceptance in society. The knowledge to choose that wardrobe with taste and refinement raised the bar further and created the need for fashion arbiters who could provide taste and refinement where customers lacked them.

Worth persuaded the empress to adopt the crinoline, and later, when he felt the style had run its course, to reject it; his designs for Eugénie and other aristocratic women, such as the Princess Pauline von Metternich, soon came to dominate French Court style. Fashionable developments among the European upper classes were driven by the rhythms of the Second Empire in France, where a week at the royal country estate Compiègne could require upward of twenty full couture ensembles, and later by the ascendance of the Prince of Wales and Princess Alexandra in England.[6] The June 22, 1905, edition of *The Lady*, an English weekly magazine for women, proclaimed, "The King and Queen [Edward VII and Alexandra] do everything in the most magnificent style and I doubt if any court in Europe can compare with ours."[7] But if taste could be set by the court, the court's taste could be set by one of the new breed of designers.

Rather than serve as mere dressmaker to the court and the wealthy citizens who swirled around it, Worth presented his designs as fait accompli. Fashion historian Valerie Steele notes, "Worth is historically important because he transformed the couture from a craft (*couture*) into a creative industry (*grande couture*), which was the predecessor to what we now know as *haute couture* . . . Worth's idea essentially consisted (and it is this that is the innovation) in asserting his authority as a creator, and proposing that women choose from a series of models."[8] Worth was not just an arbiter of fashion; in many ways, he created the fashion designer as we understand the role today, as an artistic auteur. He was also a canny businessman, who was happy to dress any woman who could afford his creations and who understood that having an actress appear onstage in a Worth gown was its own form of marketing for the house. His fame ensured that he dressed the most important actresses of the day, including Sarah Bernhardt and Eleanor Duse; he costumed Eugénie Doche as Marguerite Gautier in the original production of Dumas fils' *La Dame aux Camélias*, and the soprano Adelina Patti in *La Traviata*.[9] In fact, by the last quarter of the nineteenth century, Worth and "many of his successors counted more on dressing leading actresses on and off stage than on grande dames to publicize their designs."[10]

One of those successors was Canadian-born Lady Duff Gordon, who as the couturiere Lucile, saw her designs featured on both sides of the Atlantic.[11] Like Worth, Lucile dressed actresses; indeed, her connection to the theatre was arguably more temperamentally "natural" than Worth's. Meredith Etherington-Smith and Jeremy Pilcher note that Lucile fascinated her contemporaries because she "embodied an entirely individual sense of heightened reality."[12] The heightened reality of Lucile's designs made them an excellent medium for expressing stage character via costume onstage. The performers dressed by Lucile included British actresses Lily Elsie and Gertie Millar. Elsie made her name in musical comedies before originating the leading role in the English-language version of Franz Lehar's *The Merry Widow*, while Millar was one of the most photographed women of the Edwardian period.[13] She was the leading lady of the Gaiety Theatre, whose Gaiety Girls, the theatre's chorus, were a sensation for audiences who "fell in love with the vivacity, the superior attractiveness of face and figure, and the good breeding and grooming of the pert" chorines.[14] These actresses, and many others, were important figures in the visual culture of the day, as their images in both stage costumes and off-stage fashions were regularly reproduced in the periodical press.

Valerie Steele has argued that fashion flourishes most effectively through the interaction of knowledgeable fashion performers and spectators in a dramatic setting.¹⁵ The theatre, with its established habits of seeing both the performers onstage and fellow audience members, thus served as a prime locus for the communication of fashionable dress and bodies from the stage to audiences already engaged with the shapes and styles that were presented to them. In their study of fashion's relationship to the British theatre, Joel Kaplan and Sheila Stowell examine the Victorian and Edwardian theatre's "stage traffic" in women's bodies as well as gowns: "Upon stages like the Haymarket, the Criterion, and the St. James's . . . leading ladies not only served as living mannequins, displaying for their more affluent patrons a selection of couture house goods, but in doing so completed within the playhouses themselves a voyeuristic triangle between stage, stalls, and gallery."¹⁶ It was not just the gowns that audience members saw, however; the ensembles worn by leading ladies were inextricably connected to—literally touching—the bodies that showcased them. Actress's forms, their proportions and silhouettes, were part of what defined the fashionable look of the garments they wore.

The dramaturgy of society stages further reinforced this dynamic; the plays in the repertoire of West End London theatres frequented by wealthy and aristocratic audiences were heavily invested in visual realism, so that the onstage world of plays set in the contemporary world was easily understood as a direct reflection of the world outside the theatre.¹⁷ The nineteenth century saw an increase in visual realism fed by the confluence of a number of trends: Romantic emphasis on individuality and antiquarian interest in historical accuracy, which hastened the regular use of singular settings for each play; melodrama's appeal to fully realized spectacle; and the Well-Made Play's reliance on properties-centered dramatic devices to resolve plots. As Hugh Maguire notes, "the 'cup-and-saucer' plays supported an increased attention to details from the home environment on the stage,"¹⁸ which inevitably included dress.

Fashion is everywhere in the plays of late-nineteenth and early-twentieth-century society theatre. The plot of Wilde's *Lady Windermere's Fan* turns on a beautifully decorated evening fan being left—and seen—where it should not be. The protagonist of David Belasco's *Du Barry* is Marie Antoinette's dressmaker, and several scenes in the play take place in the milliner's shop from which the young Madame Du Barry is plucked from obscurity.¹⁹ It was also during this period that programs began to list the designers and providers of stage costumes; the program for the 1902 original production of J. M. Barrie's *The Admirable Crichton*, for example, offers the following credits: "The costumes designed by Mr. Bernard Partridge and executed by Mrs. Nettleship and Messers [*sic*] B.J. Simmons. Miss Vanbrugh's dresses by Madame Hayward. Miss Sybil Carlisle's and Miss Muriel Beaumont's by Maison Lucile."²⁰ Production photographs from the show in the collection of the Victoria and Albert Museum show all three of the leading women, who play titled sisters in the play, costumed in delicate and frothing gowns heavily trimmed in lace and tulle.²¹ The "voyeuristic triangle" of designer, actor, and audience is clearly demonstrated here: Lucile (and others) provided productions' leading ladies with couture gowns, in which audiences observed performers moving through the upper-crust worlds of society plays. The program then provided viewers with the costume designer's name, giving patrons the direction needed to acquire similar fashionable toilettes for themselves. By purchasing ensembles like those they'd seen onstage, perhaps audience members were able to bring a sense of theatricalized heighted reality into their daily lives. As Kaplan and Stowell assert, "The most obvious of obtainable goods, [gowns] could not only be admired onstage, but literally bought, carried back through the looking-glass, and made to participate in a world of social intercourse."²²

Couture gowns also played well into recurring dramatic themes of the day: appearance and essence, and whether the two meet and match, are central to play after play.²³ Playwrights found dramatic potential in the presumption that clothing did indeed make the person, so that outward appearance was presumed to equate to inner essence or figure in the consequences to individuals and society when that presumption was incorrect. Thus, onstage and in society, the stakes of presenting a body that conformed to the fashionable ideal, that looked like it *should*, to the extent that one was financially able, became all-important. Any pretensions to upward mobility depended on looking the part, and looking the part started with having the right silhouette, the right body, and the right deportment. Actresses, no less than fashion house models, sparked a desire in viewers not only to dress in the same style but to physically look the same way in the ensemble as the women they observed. The "Fashions on the Stage" column of the *Dry Goods Economist* asked its readers in 1903, "Does not the sight of a dainty show girl instil [*sic*] in the women of every city and town the desire to be as well dressed and bewitching as her sister on the other side of the footlights?"²⁴

The theatrical need for actresses' gowns to reflect the upper-class settings of their plays, showcasing a femininity at once more delicate and more sexualized than in previous decades, coincided neatly with Lucile's addition of theatrical design work to her couture output. As Kaplan and Stowell point out, "When, in the early nineties, an aging Worth began to focus his energies upon nice subtleties of cut and color, Lucile responded with calculated impudence. In 1891, she presented a collection of 'provocative' creations in a light fabric" that seemed to free dresses from the weight of heavily constructed satins and velvets. By 1897, Lucile had dressed Irene Vanbrugh in *The Liars*, produced by Charles Wyndham at his eponymously named theatre.²⁵ As Worth had done when he popularized the hoop skirt on the body of Empress Eugénie, Lucile shaped popular fashion trends using highly visible bodies as she "championed the s-bend corset with its monobosom silhouette" in commissions executed for "that most opulent of Edwardian pleasure palaces, the refurbished Gaiety [Theatre]."²⁶

The silhouettes and design details utilized by Worth, Lucile, and their contemporaries were not only seen by audiences in theatres, but theatrical costumes were increasingly anatomized in the popular press. As "play after play featured leading ladies in a sequence of the latest styles . . . journalists, as if attending a fashion show, describe[d] each ensemble with precision. . . . In February 1910, *The Play Pictorial* recorded: 'nowhere are more lovely or more fashionable frocks to be seen than on the stages of our West End theatres.'"[27] The press became a primary space of fashion description during the later nineteenth century, with paragraphs devoted to the specifics of fabric, trim, cut, color, and accessories. But it was not merely through verbal descriptions that couture ensembles and the way they were worn onstage became available to the wider public. Actress's bodies became ever-more visually available to the public during the late-nineteenth and early-twentieth centuries, as their images—in costume or in streetwear—were reproduced with great frequency in the popular press. This visibility was part of the increasing commercialization of fashion in the late nineteenth century; as urban centers grew, so did the markets for ready-made clothing at multiple price points. Although the House of Worth did not advertise in fashion journals, it had no objection to what we would today call editorial content featuring their gowns in magazines such as *Le Printemps*, *La Grande Dame*, or *The Englishwoman's Domestic Magazine* and *Harper's Bazaar*.[28] In the same way, Lucile's gowns were featured in England in *The Queen*, *The Bystander*, and British *Vogue*, and in America in *Harper's Bazaar* and *Good Housekeeping*.[29] It is telling that images of both designers' work reached as far as the relatively bourgeois *Harper's Bazaar*; it demonstrates not only the desire of that magazine's readers to access the visuals of high fashion but also the willingness of editorial gatekeepers to provide them with the images that would satisfy that desire. By the early twentieth century, the commercialization of fashion had reached a level where those lower on the socioeconomic scale were expected to engage with shifting shapes and styles and to at least aim to regularly update their wardrobes.

The couture gowns in which actresses were often pictured presented their bodies laced into corsets and padded with bustles, bust improvers, or other devices designed to alter the female form—a form that was presented as aspirational. Actresses, no less than fashion house models, created fashionable fantasies into which a woman in the audience could project herself, imagining that she "would look and act the same way if she were to wear the same clothing."[30] When Lucile gowned Lily Elsie for 1907's *The Merry Widow*, Elsie was brought to Lucile's showroom and "trained to walk with an elegant Gibson Girl glide." Lucile claimed, "There was not a movement across the stage, not a single gesture of her part . . . that we did not go through together."[31] This episode effectively demonstrates that couture designers clearly envisioned their garments as part of a totalized embodiment of femininity. To truly "wear" a gown, one not only had to don the requisite undergarments, the dress itself, and the appropriate (i.e., fashionable) accessories, but had to move with(in) the ensemble in certain ways. To be as bewitching as Gertie Millar or as striking as Lily Elsie, one had first to conform to the same bodily shape and forms of comportment, so that the desired clothing styles would hang fashionably on the figure and shift beautifully when one moved. One then had to find a way to approximate the complex shapes that made up most women's garments until World War I.

Conforming to the fashionable silhouette was made possible through the use of foundation garments expressly constructed to shape the form into the current mode. While the female form had been heavily structured by corsets (on the torso) and farthingales, panniers, and hoopskirts (from the waist down) throughout the sixteenth, seventeenth, and eighteenth centuries, the neoclassical fashions of the Napoleonic and Regency periods offered a brief respite from such uncompromisingly restrictive undergarments. With the reassertion of monarchical authority and the nineteenth-century equation of bodily control with moral rectitude, however, the strictures imposed on women's forms via their most intimate garments returned. Georges Vigarello asserts that nineteenth-century "culture multiplied its rigid procedures, the better to sculpt what was expected of the female body"; undergarments "staged" the body to accept popular forms of dress.[32] This staging changed over the course of especially the second half of the century, with the "soft, full figures" of the Second Empire (France, 1852–1870), which featured billowing busts above and hoopskirts below, giving way by the 1870s to corsets that were "longer, but also significantly more rigid . . . [not merely] enhancing a woman's curves, but . . . redefining their contours."[33] The durations of the major nineteenth-century silhouettes became progressively shorter as the century progressed.[34] These regular redefinitions of form were aided along the way by advancing technology; for example, by 1868, it was possible for corsets to be "shaped on a plaster model of a woman's torso and molded by the application of great heat."[35] The application of industrial technology to dress, traditionally more centered on handcraft work, allowed fashion designers to truly create their ideal form and then require women to adjust their own shapes to popularized designs.

Having taken as their models the images of à la mode bodies and gowns provided in the periodical press, Victorian and Edwardian women then had to reproduce on their own bodies what they saw. As images of high-society clothing became more readily available up and down the social scale, the idea that any woman could harbor some pretensions to current fashion, within her economic means, also became widespread. A macabre reminder of this is offered by the case of Mary Ann (Polly) Nichols, the first victim of Jack the

Ripper, who told a Whitechapel doorkeeper, "See what a jolly bonnet I've got now," on the night she died.[36] One solution to the quandary of how to satisfy these pretensions to fashion had developed in tandem with seasonal fashion and the illustrated press: the department store, which carried ready-to-wear garments that aped couture designs at multiple price points depending on the store.

As transportation technology improved, it also became possible to mail order ready-made garments from stores in faraway urban centers. Mail order clothing suppliers relied on the desire of women outside of large cities to keep up with changing styles and promised that their products would allow the average customer to appear in looks drawn straight from the most popular and fashionable designers of the day. Bloomingdale's *Illustrated 1886 Catalog* includes pages of women's ready-made clothing and accessories—dresses, mantels, skirts and bodices, undergarments, corsets, hosiery, and shoes—many of which required the submission of detailed measurements so that the company's in-house dressmakers could ensure proper fit. (Instructions for taking the necessary measurements are provided at the beginning of the catalog.) The catalog boasts that "neither pains nor expense are spared in securing the services of the most skillful artists, who are able to reproduce the original European designs, and competent to design models to suit the demands of this fashionable country."[37] While these built-to-measurements dresses were obviously adjustable to each customer to a certain degree, ready-made garments were not and could not be shaped to the individual in the same way that couture gowns fitted in the designer's atelier could be. Indeed, the very idea of ready-made clothing depends on a popular collective understanding of how the body of the moment is shaped: mass-produced garments, even when they could be adjusted to a woman's measurements, are based upon a set of patterns that use the same seam-line placement and general shapes for each pattern piece in a series of graded sizes. This was true of both the patterns used by commercial garment makers like Bloomingdales and of those available to the home sewer.

If there was no department store within easy travel, or if ready-made clothing remained out of reach, there was another answer for women who wanted their dresses to conform to current styles—the commercial pattern. Patterns meant for use by home dressmakers were first designed by Ellen Curtis Demorest, who sold her toiles through the magazine *Mme. Demorest's Mirror of Fashion* beginning in 1860. By 1863, Ebeneezer Butterick became the first to use tissue paper in making patterns, thereby simplifying mass production, sale, and shipment to women anywhere.[38] Worth was among those designers who developed patterns based on his designs. Primarily published in American magazines, these patterns formed a secondary income stream for the design house, but Worth also argued that "he would rather supply the pattern for a beautiful gown he created than be faced with a shockingly bad copy."[39] That is, Worth was willing to share his vision for how the female form should be shaped and embellished with women who could never afford a trip to his Paris atelier. He prioritized the accuracy of his vision of the popular form over exclusivity.

Patterns were available for dresses to suit all occasions; *The Voice of Fashion*, which produced patterns through the 1890s, included patterns for day, tea, and evening dresses, a house dress, nightgowns, drawers, and specialty ensembles like riding and tennis dresses. These were "scaled patterns that could either be copied exactly or adjusted for a customer's wants."[40] And the same 1886 Bloomingdale's catalog that spends so many pages on pictures of ready-made ensembles to be ordered also includes the "Moschowitz Model Waist Lining," a template that the home sewer could use in cutting and stitching the lining for a woman's blouse (waist). The five-piece fabric pattern includes a front, back, two-part sleeve, and collar with lines "clearly printed thereon indicating where to cut the garment, and another showing where to sew."[41] The printing of stitching lines on patterns literally instructed a woman on how to construct clothing that would shape her into the popular fashions, and body, of the day.

The twentieth-century fashion designer Christian Lacroix says, "Male couturiers in particular have always been more inspired by a fantasy image of femininity than by the structure and function of a piece of clothing designed to comfortably fit a body, serving it rather than subjugating it. Ever since Worth, male couturiers have celebrated and glorified a version of the female form that is idealized, remade, stylized."[42] These constructed forms, made fashionable by designers, the wealthy women and actresses who wore them, and the illustrated press that reproduced them, were the foundation of a popular body—a shape that was "in" for a moment in time before giving way to the next constructed silhouette. Theatre played an integral role in communicating these popular bodies as celebrity culture developed and actresses became aspirational figures.

The appearance of actresses in couture ensembles onstage provided the pretext for detailed descriptions of their gowns and images of their figures in magazines catering to a wide audience. Actresses and the wealthy women who patronized fashionable theatres could afford the best in corsetry, linens, dress fabrics and trimming, and accessories, and their bodies set the standard for the popular form. When styles of dress trickled down to the middle and lower classes (in less-costly fabrics, less-fine finishings and trims, less-closely fit lines), it was not only the style of dress that trickled down but the style of body that wore it. The theatre was a primary place of trend-setting in the late nineteenth and early twentieth centuries, and these trends included not only details of dress design and accessories but the shape of the body that wore those items, and all of these ideas were communicated to the widest possible audience through the ubiquity of actresses in the popular press. Theatre's relationship to fashion "crossed the boundaries between the public and private spheres [and] blurred distinctions between elite and popular culture."[43]

The link between fashion and the stage (or, now, the screen) is not a phenomenon limited to the late Victorian and Edwardian periods. The French actress Arletty, who in the pre–World War II years was famous for her music hall and cabaret performances, was dressed by couturiers including Poiret, Patou, and Schiaparelli.[44] Hollywood Patterns were marketed to the home sewing market in the 1940s with the images of Betty Grable, June Havoc, and Olivia de Haviland, among others.[45] And a glance through my Hollywood 2022 issue of *Vanity Fair* reveals (among just the women featured) Zendaya in Valentino, Anya Taylor-Joy wearing Tiffany & Co. jewels, and Keira Knightly in Chanel, all in ad copy; the editorial photographs include Penélope Cruz in Chanel and Nicole Kidman in Saint Laurent.[46] The stage and screen, no less than fashion houses, have always participated in celebrating various versions of the female form that are "idealized, remade, stylized."[47] The ubiquity of the material record of trickle-down couture—playtexts and theatrical ephemera; costumes, couture gowns, and readymade clothing; patterns and catalogs—offers testimony to the extent to which couture designers used the stage and actresses' bodies as part of an imagistic environment that created and communicated a popular body in the late nineteenth and early twentieth centuries. There is a tension inherent in the use of performers to stage the popular body and popular fashions. The bodies and the clothing they wear must at one and the same time feed the demand for what is already popular—they must be au courant in order to be taken seriously as engaged with the current fashionable mode—while also retaining the power to present the embodied shapes and styles that will (re)create the new, next popular bodies and fashions. In the late Victorian and Edwardian periods, these stylized, remade forms became visually ubiquitous via the illustrated popular press and helped create the modern paradigm of a popular body to which any woman could aspire.

Notes

1. Jean-Phillipe's older brother Gaston had already joined the firm a year earlier, in a more heavily administrative role. Chantal Troubert-Tollu, Francoise Tetart-Vittu, Jean-Marie Martin-Hattembergy, and Fabrice Olivieri, *The House of Worth, 1858–1954: The Birth of Haute-Couture* (London: Thames and Hudson, 2017), 6.

2. Chantal Troubert-Tollu et al., *The House of Worth, 1858–1954: The Birth of Haute-Couture* (London: Thames and Hudson, 2017), 94.

3. In arguing for an expansive understanding of how the material and performative archive may be read, I borrow from Diana Taylor, among others.

Diana Taylor, *The Archive and the Repertoire: Performing Cultural Memory in the Americas* (Durham, NC: Duke University Press, 2003).

4. Jessica Krick, "Charles Frederick Worth (1825–1895) and the House of Worth," Metropolitan Museum of Art (website), accessed March 27, 2022.

5. See Quentin Bell's *On Human Finery* (1949) (London: Hogarth Press, rev. ed., 1976). Bell applies Thorsten Veblen's ideas of conspicuous consumption, conspicuous leisure, and conspicuous waste specifically to dress; see Veblen's "The Theory of the Leisure Class," *Journal of Political Economy* 7, no. 4 (September 1899): 425–55.

6. "upward of twenty full couture ensembles": Valerie Steele, "Capital of Luxury and Fashion," in *Paris: Capital of Fashion* (New York: Bloomsbury, 2019), 116–37, e-book accessed on Bloomsbury Collections, March 3, 2022.

7. Valerie D. Mendes and Amy de la Haye, *Lucile, Ltd: London, Paris, New York and Chicago, 1890s–1930s* (London: V and A Publishing, 2009), 15.

8. Steele, "Capital of Luxury and Fashion."

9. Trubert-Tollu et al., *The House of Worth, 1858–1954*, 67.

10. Mary Lynn Stewart, *Dressing Modern Frenchwomen: Marketing Haute Couture, 1919–1939* (Baltimore, MD: Johns Hopkins University Press, 2008), 23.

11. Mendes and de la Haye, *Lucile, Ltd.*, 185, 192. Lucile is also often credited with borrowing directly from theatrical convention to invent the modern fashion show, a parade of models wearing her designs: "These personal theatres of fashion were played out beneath scaled-down proscenium arches. . . . Emulating theatre programs, leaflets were printed with the running order of her fashion parades" (Mendes and de la Haye, *Lucile, Ltd.*, 185).

12. Meredith Etherington-Smith and Jeremy Pilcher, *The 'It' Girls: Lucy, Lady Duff Gordon, the Couturiere 'Lucile,' and Elinor Glynn, the Romantic Novelist* (London: H. Hamilton, 1986), xiii.

13. Sydney Higgins, "Gertie Millar (1879–1952)," The Golden Age of British Theatre (1880–1920 (website), accessed March 3, 2022.

14. Cecil Smith and Glenn Litton, *Musical Comedy in America* (New York: Theatre Arts Books, 1981), 64.

15. Valerie Steele, "The Theatre of Fashion," *Paris: Capital of Fashion* (New York: Bloomsbury, 2019).

16. Joel H. Kaplan and Sheila Stowell, *Theatre and Fashion: Oscar Wilde to the Suffragettes* (Cambridge: Cambridge University Press, 1994), 2.

17. See, for example, Bert O. States, *Great Reckonings in Little Rooms* (Berkeley: University of California Press, 1985), and Hugh Maguire, "The Victorian Theatre as a Home from Home," *Journal of Design History* 13, no. 2 (2000): 110.

18. Hugh Maguire, "The Victorian Theatre as a Home from Home," *Journal of Design History* 13, no. 2 (2000): 110.

19. Garff B. Wilson, *Three Hundred Years of American Drama and Theatre: From "Ye Bare and Ye Cubb" to "Hair"* (Englewood Cliffs, NJ: Prentice-Hall, 1973), 287–96. So connected was the plotting of the play to the fashionable world outside the theatre that for the 1902 revival of the play that opened the Belasco Theatre in New York, women in the audience were given a souvenir booklet that included photographs of the actors in (period) costume.

20. Ian Riches, "Delving into the Archives at J. M. Barrie's Birthplace," National Trust for Scotland (website), accessed April 27, 2022.

21. Photographs in McCarrolls's collection, taken of unnumbered theatrical ephemera in the clippings collections of the Victoria and Albert Museum, Blythe House, London, January 2011.

22. Kaplan and Stowell, *Theatre and Fashion*, 11.

23. George Rowell, *The Victorian Theatre, 1792–1914: A Survey* (Cambridge: Cambridge University Press, 1978), 138. Kaplan and Stowell also discuss numerous theatrical productions that focused in title, characters, and/or setting on some element of the fashion industry or dress in society.

24. "Fashions on the Stage," *Dry Goods Economist* (May 23, 1903), 23, quoted in Nancy J. Troy, "The Theatre of Fashion: Staging Haute Couture in Early 20th-Century France," *Theatre Journal* 53 (2001): 1.

25. Kaplan and Stowell, *Theatre and Fashion*, 39–40.

26. Kaplan and Stowell, *Theatre and Fashion*, 115.

27. Mendes and de la Haye, *Lucile, Ltd.*, 185.

28. Trubert-Tollu et al., *The House of Worth, 1858–1954*, 30, 200.

29. Mendes and de la Haye, *Lucile, Ltd.* (London: Victoria and Albert Publishing, 2009), 10.

30. Troy, "The Theatre of Fashion," 1.

31. Kaplan and Stowell, *Theatre and Fashion*, 115.

32. Georges Vigarello, "The Nineteenth Century: From Artifice to Anonymity," in *Fashioning the Body: An Intimate History of the Silhouette*, ed. Denis Bruna (New Haven, CT: Yale University Press, 2015), 153.

33. Aurore Bayle-Loudet, "The Corset: Essential Protagonist of Modern Femininity," in *Fashioning the Body: An Intimate History of the Silhouette*, ed. Denis Bruna (New Haven, CT: Yale University Press, 2015), 164.

34. In rough terms: Slim neoclassical lines prevailed for the first twenty-five years of the century, with billowing Romantic sleeves and skirts on either side of a slightly raised waist characterizing the second quarter of the century. The domed crinoline (hoopskirt) dominated the silhouette of the 1850s and early 1860s before its fullness began to shift to the rear of the body. In the late 1860s and 1870s, this shift was coupled by a lengthening of the corseted torso and a narrowing of necklines and sleeves. By 1875, these trends had solidified in the first iteration of the bustle silhouette, with extreme projections of the skirt to the back of the body. This extreme fullness collapsed into the "natural

form" silhouette with a tight cuirass bodice and slim skirt for a brief time in the early 1880s, before returning with a vengeance in the last years of the decade. The 1890s were marked by the expansion of the sleeve into enormous leg o'mutton shoulders by 1895 and then a narrowing by the turn of the century; these sleeves, whether slim or full, were part of masculine-inspired tailored bodices, blouses, or waists, worn over bell-shaped skirts. This shape was constructed by heavily boned hourglass corsets. The silhouette and fabrics of womenswear softened in the first years of the twentieth century, as the hourglass gave way to the s-bend Edwardian corset, which extended over the hip girdle and created a monobosom, pigeon-breasted bust. Skirts collapsed into a trumpet shape, with fullness below the knees, and delicate "lingerie" gowns were increasingly made out of delicate laces and chiffons.

35. Bayle-Loudet, "The Corset," 166.

36. Hallie Rubenhold, *The Five: The Untold Lives of the Women Killed by Jack the Ripper* (Boston: Houghton Mifflin Harcourt, 2019), 71.

37. Bloomingdale Brothers, *Bloomingdale's Illustrated 1886 Catalog: Fashion, Dry Goods and Housewares* (New York: Dover Publications, 1988), 3.

38. Vintage Fashion Guild (website), "Vintage Patterns," accessed March 3, 2022.

39. Troubert-Tollu et al., *The House of Worth, 1858–1954*, 30.

40. Kristina Harris, ed., *Authentic Victorian Fashion Patterns: A Complete Ladies Wardrobe* (Mineola, NY: Dover Publications, 1999), np.

41. Bloomingdale Brothers, *Bloomingdale's Illustrated 1886 Catalog*, 153.

42. Christian Lacroix, "Forward," in Trubert-Tollu et al., *The House of Worth, 1858–1954: The Birth of Haute-Couture* (London: Thames and Hudson, 2017), 7.

43. Troy, "The Theatre of Fashion," 4.

44. Stewart, *Dressing Modern Frenchwomen*, 23.

45. "Vintage Movie Star Patterns," So Vintage (website), accessed March 28, 2022.

46. *Vanity Fair*, no. 736, "Hollywood 2022," Zendaya, 24–25, Taylor-Joy, 29, Knightly, 41, and Cruz and Kidman, 74–75.

47. Lacroix, "Forward," 7.

Trauma from a Safe Distance

The Unprecedented Success of *The History of the Troubles (Accordin' to My Da)*

Eleanor Owicki

IN JULY 2010, I arrived in Belfast, Northern Ireland, as a newly minted PhD candidate on my first real dissertation research trip. As we left the airport, I told my taxi driver that I was there to study theatre. He excitedly told me about a show that had made a significant impression on him: Martin Lynch, Conor Grimes, and Alan McKee's *A History of the Troubles (Accordin' to My Da)*. Directed by Karl Wallace, the play had premiered at the Cathedral Quarter Arts Festival (CQAF) in 2002 (eight years before this conversation took place). My driver explained that he wasn't a regular theatregoer but had seen the play three times because he felt it represented his experience of the Northern Irish Troubles (1968–1998) in a way no other depiction had.

My driver was not alone in his affection for the play, which sold out an extended run at the CQAF in May 2002 and was revived at the Grand Opera House the following January. It was revived again in 2004, 2007, 2009, 2010, 2011, and 2013, always with the same cast. These revivals included additional performances in Belfast (generally at the Grand Opera House), as well as tours covering Northern Ireland, the Republic of Ireland, and London. In 2016, Lynch, Grimes, and McKee penned a sequel: *The History of the Peace (Accordin' to My Ma)*. While not as successful as its predecessor, it was revived at the Grand Opera House in 2018. The enduring popularity of *The History of the Troubles* would have been unusual for a play in any location and was certainly unique in the history of Belfast theatre.

In this article, I explore the reason for this unprecedented success. Some of this was certainly due to the play's quality. It was fast-paced and funny, particularly when performed by actors with strong comedic talents, as the initial production and revivals were. But this alone would not be enough to explain its long-standing appeal, especially to people who like my taxi driver were not in the habit of attending the theatre. I therefore argue that a great deal of the play's success grew from its ability to package the Troubles into a manageable and relatively detached narrative; it also provided a sense of a new beginning that was primarily optimistic but still tinged with some skepticism. Throughout, it sought to construct a comfortable familiarity rooted in shared experience. This mood appealed primarily to audiences who had lived through the Troubles and were eager to receive some sense of closure.

The Play and Its Creators

As the title suggests, *The History of the Troubles (Accordin' to My Da)* provided a rapid and chaotic summary of the violence that gripped Northern Ireland between roughly 1968 and 1998. Briefly, this was a conflict between three major groups: republican paramilitaries (mostly Catholic), loyalist paramilitaries (mostly Protestant), and the state forces of Northern Ireland and the UK (particularly the army and the police). There were two major issues: first, whether the Protestant unionists (who made up a slight majority) would continue to maintain power by limiting the civil rights of Catholic nationalists; second, whether Northern Ireland would remain a part of the United Kingdom or join the Republic of Ireland. As time passed, these motivations became further complicated by cycles of trauma and vengeance. During this thirty-year period, more than 3,600 people were killed and countless more were physically or psychologically wounded. The conflict largely ended with the Good Friday Agreement (GFA) of 1998, which was first agreed on by the combatants and politicians and then approved in a referendum by the population of Northern Ireland.

The History of the Troubles compressed this period into seventy-five minutes, presenting it from the perspective of one man, Gerry Courtney (played by actor and broadcaster Ivan Little). Gerry was joined onstage by a host of friends, family, and acquaintances, all played by the comic duo of Conor Grimes and Alan McKee (who cowrote the script with Lynch). This was the second collaboration between the three; they had previously created a piece with a similar structure focusing on the history of Rathlin Island (off Northern Ireland's northeast coast). *The History of the Troubles* was darkly comic, acknowledging the trauma of the conflict without wallowing in it, as well as balancing cynicism with heartfelt emotion. The play both began and ended with Gerry at the hospital waiting for news of a birth (first of his son, then of his grandson) while political events spiraled in the streets outside. The primary shift was in the mood of those events; they were tragic as he waited for the birth of his son and joyous as he awaited his grandson.

Between them, Grimes and McKee played more than thirty characters. Many were brief—appearing for under thirty seconds and then never returning. Some of these were generic characters, such as newsreaders, a prison warder, and a barman. Two real-life figures also made quick appearances: Jack

Lynch, the Republic of Ireland's Taoiseach (prime minister) when the Troubles began, and John DeLorean, whose eponymous cars were manufactured in Northern Ireland. Significantly, neither was especially important within the Northern Irish conflict. More prominent (and frequently caricatured) figures like Gerry Adams and Ian Paisely did not appear. Grimes's and McKee's more significant characters were Gerry's friends and neighbors, creating a snapshot of his community. Finally, the pair played Derek and Seamus, narrators who moved the audience through the events of both the Troubles and Gerry's personal life.

The play's staging emphasized the virtuosity of the performers (particularly Grimes and McKee). David Craig's design was simple. Its most striking element was "a backdrop of photographs depicting Ulster's highs and lows—there a burned out bus, here a portrait of Van the Man. It's a wonderful kaleidoscope of landmarks which have formed battle-scarred Belfast."[1] The only other set pieces were a chair and three stools. All three performers mimed most of the props and wore dark, neutral costumes with no changes. This meant that Grimes and McKee's many character shifts were signaled exclusively through the actors' vocal and physical performances. These tended toward broad comedy rather than nuanced realism. The lack of clear visual distinction between the characters and the rapidity of the changes also contributed to the play's chaotic feeling. Grimes's and McKee's frenetic whirlwind of characters mirrored the political turmoil surrounding Gerry.

Rock and pop songs provided another through line (sometimes sung by the actors and sometimes in recordings by the original artists). The Rolling Stones featured particularly prominently, and even Rick Astley's "Never Gonna Give You Up" made an appearance (although the show's premiere predated the phenomenon of "Rickrolling" by several years). Early in the play, the audience did hear the republican folk song "The Men Behind the Wire," but otherwise the music was entirely popular and apolitical. Although this play was far from being a jukebox musical, these songs did fulfill a similar function by encouraging nostalgia in audiences from both sides of the sectarian division. The use of music in this way has become a staple of Lynch's plays, where songs provide joyful moments of shared experience for audiences and characters.

Although the play is credited to all three authors, news coverage and scholarship have generally treated it as Lynch's play. Martin Lynch has had a long-standing and significant career in Northern Irish theatre. In 1976, he cofounded the Turf Lodge Fellowship Community Theatre and first achieved success in professional theatre with his 1981 play *Dockers* at the Lyric Theatre. This was followed by plays including *The Interrogation of Ambrose Fogarty* (1982), *Castles in the Air* (1983), and *Pictures of Tomorrow* (1995). By 2002, when *The History of the Troubles* premiered, he had also been involved in several other significant collaborations. He worked with the all-female

Charabanc company at its founding, cowriting their first play, *Lay Up Your Ends* in 1983. Following community devising workshops, he and Marie Jones cowrote *The Wedding Community Play* in 1999, and in 2000 he contributed a scene to *convictions*, a highly influential site-specific work staged in Belfast's decommissioned Crumlin Road Courthouse.

In retrospect, the end of the conflict marked a turning point in Lynch's career. In the 1980s and 1990s, he had made a name as an explicitly socialist and republican playwright (although he was a member of the Official IRA, which rejected the violent campaign carried out by the Provisional IRA and other republican paramilitary organizations). Following the GFA, however, he moved into a style that one might describe as more broadly humanist. His role "as a potent and often controversial articulator of the voice of working-class Belfast" remained constant, however.[2] Lynch continued to center the working class as both the subject of his plays and his target audience. Indeed, in 2014 he raised controversy when he spoke in front of the Northern Ireland Assembly's Committee for Culture, Arts, and Leisure and criticized Belfast's new MAC Arts Centre as elitist and hostile to those not already immersed in the arts.[3] In the years following the GFA, he also moved into directing and producing, but throughout he strove to present plays reflecting working-class stories to working-class audiences.

While less prominent in the coverage of the play, its other two authors (who made up two-thirds of the cast) were also essential to its popularity. Although each is a successful actor in his own right, Grimes and McKee have particularly come to be known through their work together. As performers, they appeared in the "Male Toilets" section of *convictions*. In Daragh Carville's darkly comic piece, the two played a photographer (Grimes) and a journalist (McKee) who feared the new peace would decrease international interest in Northern Ireland. They came up with a plan to stage bombings—only during the tourism offseason—to keep the state in the public consciousness.[4] Although Grimes and McKee did not write this piece, it demonstrated the style of irreverent, dark humor for which they would come to be known. They continued to work together as writers after *The History of the Troubles*. For example, they penned and starred in Christmas shows at the Lyric Theatre: adult alternatives to the more family-oriented pantomimes. Thus, like Lynch, the pair were well-established figures on the Belfast theatre scene who already had a broad appeal.

A Moment of Transition

In the years following the GFA, there was a push to define a "New Northern Ireland" and a "New Belfast." Rhetoric of rebirth and renewal was rife. This involved creating as much distance as possible from the "bad old days" and working to counter an ever-present anxiety that the conflict wasn't really in the past. Although the GFA did drastically improve life in Northern Ireland and usher in a more peaceful era, these concerns were not unfounded. The deadliest attack of the conflict—the Omagh bombing, which killed twenty-nine and injured hundreds more—occurred about three months after the ratification of the GFA. Similarly, the GFA was often vague about the exact systems that would ensure its mandates; these continued to be sites of bitter debate for many years after. Lynch directly linked *The History of the Troubles* to this moment of ambiguous transition. In an interview about the play, he observed: "The old Northern Ireland has gone. The building of the new one is going on right before our eyes. It's like the new building is still covered in scaffolding and sacking and we can't see what it looks like—yet."[5] This encompasses much of the feeling of the moment: hope for improvement coupled with the anxiety about entering a new, unknown landscape.

The play most clearly expressed this ambivalence with its use of a double ending. First, the chorus of two summarized the conflict's end on the larger political level. Shortly thereafter the audience saw what this ending meant for Gerry. In the former scene, Grimes and McKee appeared for their final moment as narrators Derek and Seamus. They observed:

> DEREK: So, The Troubles were now officially over.
> SEAMUS: Unless of course, you were on the wrong end of a knee capping . . .
> DEREK: . . . Or your children attended the Holy Cross Primary . . .
> SEAMUS: . . . Or you live in interface areas . . .
> DEREK: . . . Or you were out shopping in Omagh one Saturday afternoon.
> SEAMUS: But apart from all the bombings . . .
> DEREK: . . And the shootings and maimings, the Troubles were over.[6]

Here, the characters highlighted events undermining the narrative that the GFA marked a perfect break between violence and peace. Some of these incidents had garnered international attention, including the Omagh bombing and the 2001 Holy Cross dispute, when residents of a Protestant residential area abusively protested Catholic children attending school in their neighborhood. Derek and Seamus also referenced the smaller-scale attacks that received considerably less attention. In particular, "knee-capping" alluded to the prevalence of so-called punishment beatings that paramilitaries continued to use to control the behavior of "their own side." This small-scale violence also included disturbances in places where Catholic and Protestant neighborhoods met ("interface areas"). The picture presented by this exchange was far from one of peace and harmony. While life might be better than during the conflict, it was certainly not perfect.

The play's actual ending struck a more utopian note, however. Gerry expressed more optimism about the future—for both his family and Northern Ireland—than had Derek and Seamus. In the play's final moments, Gerry met his infant grandson. This mirrored the play's opening, when Gerry had waited for Colm's birth. However, it no longer felt that the rest of the world was falling apart around him. In the play's final lines, Gerry told his grandson, "You're startin' with a completely new sheet, eh? You're one big blank page, that's what you are. But you're the next page, our kid . . . you're the next page."[7] Here, Gerry voiced the widely held hope that a new post-GFA generation would be able to move forward free of the traumas and prejudices of its past. As Jane Coyle summarized in her review in the *Irish Times*, "Through laughter and tears, the audience is invited to share in Gerry's individual experience and to echo his hope that his new-born grandson, the next page in the family album, will have a different story written upon his young life."[8] Perhaps surprisingly, these two endings were not presented as contradictory; while there was certainly a tension between them, the script did not suggest that one needed to be more true than the other. Gerry's sentimental ending probably carried more weight for audiences, since it was the play's final moment and was tied to the main character's specific story (it was certainly more likely to be mentioned in reviews). Overall, however, the coexistence of these two endings expressed the complex mixture of hope and cynicism surrounding the end of the conflict.

The news coverage of *The History of the Troubles* was keen to connect the play with the "New Northern Ireland," using it to define a turning point in Northern Irish theatre. Reporters and artists alike were quick to distinguish the play from earlier "Troubles drama," a genre that they either implied or explicitly stated was hackneyed, sentimental, and irrelevant to the experiences of those who had actually lived through the conflict. For example, Lynch commented, "the BBC drama department killed off Troubles drama by churning out worn piles of shite that had no credibility."[9] Similarly, Jane Coyle wrote in a review: "This is the play about the Troubles that Lynch has shied away from writing, until now. This is no folksy piece of nostalgia, no depressing saga of bombs and bullets. This is the genuine article, written with humour and humanity, out of unashamedly personal experience, with no tipping of the cap to headline news, political correctness or balance."[10] In Coyle's view, this genre of "Troubles drama" either avoided dealing with the trauma of the period ("folksy nostalgia") or was unremittingly bleak, probably with little effort to include anything not directly tied to the conflict (a "depressing saga of bombs and bullets"). Clearly, she admired Lynch's ability to find a middle ground between these two extremes.

Coyle's review also framed the play firmly as a part of the "New Northern Ireland" by suggesting that *The History of the Troubles*'s ability to avoid these tropes was not solely due to its creator's talent. She implied that the conflict had previously limited Lynch's options and that this play could only be written in the "New Northern Ireland." In several interviews, Lynch echoed this sentiment, describing the play as his "full stop on the Troubles" after which he would move on.[11] This didn't end up being the case, since his 2009 play *The Chronicles of Long Kesh* offered a similarly frenetic trip through the history of the conflict (this time from the perspectives of inmates and guards at Northern Ireland's most famous prison). However, this insistence helped frame the play as part of a transition not only for Northern Ireland but for Lynch himself.

The contexts in which the play was produced also helped to shape the meanings it held for audiences. It premiered in 2002 as part of the Cathedral Quarter Arts Festival (CQAF), which had first been held in 2000. In contrast, the Belfast Festival, the city's most prominent arts festival, had been running since 1962. The CQAF was designed to support the redevelopment of the newly christened "Cathedral Quarter" (just to the northeast of the city center) into a focal point for arts and culture as well as a destination for evening events. During the conflict, most nightlife had remained extremely local; few residents were interested in or felt safe venturing into the city center. This did not change immediately after the conflict. As Roisin Ingle noted in a feature ahead of the first festival: "One minute the city streets are full of shoppers, workers and schoolchildren and the next minute the arteries around City Hall are deserted. A local says people tend to stay away from the city center at night: 'It's a throwback to the Troubles.'"[12] Festival director Sean Kelly hoped that the CQAF and the Cathedral Quarter more generally would help to change this: "If it is about anything, this festival is about reclaiming the city centre for all citizens of Belfast. . . . We are trying to re-imagine the city centre as the thriving, integrated, cosmopolitan place it was at one time."[13] Thus, the area and the festival were both central to the "New Northern Ireland" project, reinforcing the image of a globalized, sophisticated city that Belfast hoped to present on the world stage.

The later transfer to the Grand Opera House also helped solidify the show's popularity, although this venue carried very different associations than the CQAF. The building, which sits near the city center, was built in 1895. It would therefore be difficult to describe it as part of the "New Northern Ireland." Instead, it supported the play's goals by welcoming the working-class audiences that Lynch most wanted to reach. In its current iteration, the Grand Opera House is primarily a presenting rather than a producing venue. When large musicals tour through Belfast, they generally perform here. It is also the site of the city's largest pantomime, a beloved holiday tradition in the UK.

As such, the Grand Opera House draws a very different audience than the Lyric, the city's largest producing theatre. The Lyric sits in the city's south, near Queen's University. This location, along with the venue's focus on more "serious drama," means that it attracts an audience more heavily made up of middle-class regular theatregoers. Staging the play at the Grand Opera House, therefore, aligned it with the venue's tradition of popular, commercial theatre.

Still, *The History of the Troubles* could easily have been a divisive play. Lynch was certainly aware of this possibility. In an interview before the play's premiere, he said, "There may be people saying that this is another Fenian's [a derogatory term for a Catholic] take on the Troubles, but that would be a petty-minded response. Those who know my work would be aware that there has never been any sectarian content and those who don't will just have to come along and judge for themselves."[14] Here, Lynch made a distinction between theatre that focuses on only one community and theatre that expresses sectarian arguments or beliefs. Lynch is from the nationalist community, as is the play's main character. Many audience members might therefore have expected the play to endorse a nationalist narrative of the conflict. The play was far less interested in explaining why the Troubles had happened or assigning blame for them, however, than it was in showing how these major events had shaped one man's life. This increased the play's potential audience significantly.

The play was less successful when it left Ireland, however. *The History of the Troubles* presented many of the most significant points of the conflict's history and therefore had the potential to teach those who had not directly experienced it. Reviewer Robert McMillan described the play as "a whistle-stop tour, one man's history lesson presented through a funfair mirror."[15] Lynch endorsed the idea of the play as a vehicle for teaching: "The play offers a quirky and humorous insight into the story of the troubles, . . . As a history lesson, it's much more effective than any academic book or television documentary!"[16] In spite of this potential, the play was less successful with audiences more removed from the conflict. Tim Miles notes that "*The History of the Troubles (Accordin' to My Da)* was a dismal failure when it was performed in England. At the Tricycle, despite having the same cast as the Belfast production, it played to tiny audiences and was largely savaged by the critics." Miles goes on to quote dismissive comments from several London critics, who described the play as a "feeble, coarse comedy" and a "lumbering triviality."[17] These critics evidently felt that the subject needed to be treated with more solemnity and that the use of humor made the play less artistically worthy. One might speculate that London audiences would have been more comfortable with a play that more closely conformed to the melodramatic tropes of "Troubles drama" against which the play was actively working. Certainly the differences between the play's reception in the two cities demonstrate the importance of audience to its success.

A Hapless Everyman

The play's popularity in Belfast (and perhaps lack thereof in London) was also largely due its main character's relationship (or lack thereof) with politics. Not only did Gerry begin the play with a lack of interest in politics, but he also arguably became even more distanced from them as the play progressed. Reviews underscored Gerry's apolitical, even passive nature. They described him as "an everyman," as "blown about and up by the winds of the change," and as "try[ing] to get on with normal family life."[18] Terms such as "decent," "ordinary," and "hapless" also appeared frequently. Little, who played Gerry, was quoted as saying: "Gerry's not a political character, and he has no axe to grind. He's just an ordinary man caught in extraordinary circumstances, and although he's from west Belfast, he gets annoyed with his own side as well as the other, then gets interned because he's just in the wrong place at the wrong time."[19] Coyle described Little's performance as "a man confused and hapless in the face of a growing storm of circumstance."[20] Gerry was more a spectator to the conflict than a participant, allowing the audience to relive this history from a safe distance.

The casting of Little in this role also helped create a sense of familiarity and safety for the audience. In addition to being an actor, Little had been a news reporter for Ulster Television since 1980. During this time, he had become a trusted household name for whom many on both sides of the sectarian divide felt deep affection. His stage appearances included the Grand Opera House's pantomime in 1997, a prime example of popular, apolitical theatre. This affection for "Big" Ivan Little was reflected in the news coverage about his participation in the show. Here, the reports were at their coziest. For example, multiple newspaper pieces reported on the debates that had apparently happened within the production about whether Little should shave off his signature beard (it was eventually decided that he should not). One such article was titled "A Very Hairy Situation!: TV Ivan's Close Shave with the Troubles."[21] The facetious solemnity with which commentators approached this issue suggested that nothing about the play needed to be taken too seriously.

Gerry's only direct encounter with the conflict was early in the play when he was interned on suspicion of being a member of the IRA. In fact, he and his friend Felix had gone to a bar to inquire about joining. It was obvious that their naiveté about what being members of this organization would actually entail made them poor candidates, however. The IRA recruiter had already dismissed them as potential members by the time the police raided the bar and arrested everyone. Although several scenes took place while Gerry and Felix were imprisoned in Long Kesh, the focus was more on the boredom of their existence and their separation from their families than on political events inside or outside the prison. After his release, Gerry made no effort to rejoin the republican movement (or indeed any other political cause).

Throughout the play, politics and the events of the Troubles came second to the events of Gerry's own life. In one notable scene approximately halfway through the play, Gerry lay in the hospital having his hemorrhoids treated while being updated on news of the hunger strike being carried out by republican prisoners at Long Kesh (in which ten men would eventually die). While Gerry was moved by this news, his focus remained, quite literally, on the pain in his rear. Gerry's self-centeredness here did not make him unlikeable. There was a charm in his bumbling, and his lack of interest in politics meant that the play did not need to rehash the debates from that particular moment. The hunger strikes were a time of intense emotion and trauma, particularly among nationalist communities, but this treatment gave audiences a certain degree of distance from these memories.

In addition, this sequence offered an example of the ways *The History of the Troubles* actively worked against the tropes of Troubles drama. As Ingle noted, the Royal Victoria Hospital, where this scene (as well as the opening and closing scenes) took place, is "a potent symbol of Northern Ireland's bloody history."[22] In most narratives set during the Troubles, use of this location would have focused on its role in treating victims of the conflict. Even if the main character was at the hospital for a non-conflict-related reason (as Gerry was), one would have expected him to see and comment on other patients who were victims of violence. This was not the case, however. While at the hospital for his hemorrhoids, Gerry spoke with Fireball, the hospital porter who always knew everything happening in the hospital and was now working in its morgue. This could have provided him an opportunity to discuss the horrific damage done to the bodies he saw. He never mentioned their cause of death or visible injuries, however. Instead, he focused on how he had overcome his anxiety of working around dead bodies by naming them all after jockeys on whom he had lost money (poorly chosen bets on horse races were an ongoing facet of this character).

Gerry's relationship with "the other side" was similarly left vague. Like most working-class Belfast residents, Gerry primarily interacted with those within his own sectarian community. Spatial and educational segregation in the city has meant that this was generally not an active choice. Most of the people Gerry encountered on a day-to-day basis would also have been Catholics, and he would have needed to actively seek out connections with Protestants. While Gerry never did this, he also never expressed anti-Protestant sentiments. The only character explicitly identified as Protestant was Gerry's former colleague Benny, who only appeared for one short scene. Although the two men hadn't stayed in touch, they expressed fondness for each other, quickly falling into a routine of friendly teasing. Benny assured Gerry that their other former colleagues miss him, rejecting Gerry's assumption that they were glad to be rid of "that Fenian so-and-so!"[23] The interaction was brief and lacked the high stakes that would accompany a meeting between members of the two communities in most "Troubles drama." The men neither fought nor did they lament that the sectarian divide had ruined their friendship. It was a perfectly pleasant moment that for the most part might have occurred between former work acquaintances anywhere.

When tragedy did strike Gerry's life, it occurred in a way that further distanced *The History of the Troubles* from the cliches of Troubles drama. Late in the play, Gerry's son Colm was beaten to death in the street. The surrounding context made this especially tragic. Colm was early in his studies at Queen's University, a source of great pride for his parents. In addition, the attack took place just after Colm had left his sister Grainne's wedding reception (indeed, Gerry learned of his death while still celebrating). Contrary to what one might have expected, however, the attack was unrelated to the larger conflict. In many narratives set during the Troubles (including the ones from which Lynch was trying to distance his play), Colm would either have died as a result of his own involvement in paramilitary activity or would have been an innocent victim attacked by paramilitaries for being from "the wrong side." In *The History of the Troubles*, however, the attack was purely random without any apparent connection to sectarianism (Colm's ghost briefly appeared and told Gerry "They didn't like my hair or something").[24] Colm's death served as a reminder that the conflict had not controlled all aspects of life during the Troubles. People continued to live and die in ways that had nothing to do with the larger political situation.

Conclusion

The History of the Troubles navigated a precarious path: It reviewed traumatic events without retraumatizing audience members, provided humor without being disrespectful, and balanced optimism with the knowledge of just how easily things could go wrong. The play's unprecedented popularity in Northern Ireland shows that it largely succeeded in this. In particular, its appeal to those who were not regular theatregoers (including my taxi driver) suggests that it truly did offer something that both was new and addressed a need in the audience. As is to be expected, however, the play was not universally popular, even in Northern Ireland. For instance, theatre scholar Mark Phelan argues that it and Lynch's later play *Chronicles of Long Kesh* lack real engagement, since "at no stage . . . are the politics, ethics, and aftermath of political violence considered."[25] This criticism feels more relevant to *Chronicles of Long Kesh*, however, since that play dealt much more closely with those who had been involved in the conflict. Many of the characters in the later play were in prison because they had carried out violent attacks, but the play rarely dealt with the impact of these events on victims or their families. In *The History of the Troubles*, however, the omission of this analysis was a direct result of Lynch's choice to focus on a main character whose life had not been directly impacted by the conflict.

Given all of this, perhaps it is not surprising that the play was less successful with London audiences. Although the artists suggested that the play could act as a history lesson on the Troubles, Gerry's political detachment meant that the conflict's major events were only mentioned in passing. The more violent attacks of the conflict—whether carried out by paramilitaries or government security forces—generally did not even receive a mention. There was simply not enough information or context for the play to successfully provide an overview of the conflict to audiences who didn't already understand it. In contrast, Belfast audiences had no need for such a lesson, nor did they need to be convinced of the severity of the Troubles. For those who had lived through these events, the references that were included helped to establish a timeline against which Gerry lived his mundane life. Thus, the play offered Belfast audiences a reminder not so much of the conflict as of the fact that life had gone on throughout it. It also offered the promise that, to whatever extent "normality" returned, life would continue to go on.

Notes

1. Grania McFadden, "Subtle, Slapstick . . . Lynch's Wonderful Kaleidescope," *Belfast Telegraph*, May 3, 2002.

2. Neil Johnston, "Interview: Martin's Lynchpins," *Belfast Telegraph*, March 9, 2002.

3. Committee for Culture, Arts, and Leisure, "Inquiry into Inclusion in the Arts of Working-Class Communities: Martin Lynch," *Northern Ireland Assembly* (website), May 27, 2014.

4. Daragh Carville, "Male Toilets," in *convictions*, 32–37. Tinderbox Theatre, 2000.

5. Quoted in Robert McMillen, "A New Riot through the Troubles," *Irish News*, May 2, 2002.

6. Martin Lynch, Conor Grimes, and Alan McKee, *The History of the Troubles (Accordin' to My Da)* (Belfast, Northern Ireland: Lagan Press, 2005), 67–68.

7. Lynch, Grimes, and McKee, *The History of the Troubles (Accordin' to My Da)*, 69.

8. Jane Coyle, "The History of the Troubles (Accordin' To My Da)," *Irish Times*, May 4, 2002.

9. Quoted in Róisín Ingle, "Lighting Fires in the Belly," *Irish Times*, April 29, 2002.

10. Coyle, "The History of the Troubles (Accordin' To My Da)."

11. See, for example, Geoff Hill, "According to My Da, This Man Used to Be a Reporter," *Belfast News Letter*, May 2, 2002.

12. Roisin Ingle, "Belfast's Heart Begins to Beat," *Irish Times*, April 27, 2000.

13. Quoted in Ingle, "Belfast's Heart Begins to Beat."

14. Ingle, "Lighting Fires in the Belly."

15. McMillen, "A New Riot through the Troubles."

16. McMillen, "A New Riot through the Troubles."

17. Tim Miles, "'Pack up Your Troubles and Smile, Smile, Smile': Comic Plays about the Legacy of 'the Troubles,'" *Comedy Studies* 1, no. 1 (January 2010): 53. Miles had special insight into the play's sojourn in London, having been working at the Tricycle's box office at the time.

18. Ian Hill, "Review: Humour Brought to a Troubled History," *Belfast News Letter*, January 29, 2003.

19. Hill, "According to My Da, This Man Used to Be a Reporter."

20. Coyle, "The History of the Troubles (Accordin' to My Da)."

21. Sue Corbett, "A Very Hairy Situation!: TV Ivan's Close Shave with the Troubles," *Belfast Telegraph*, April 21, 2002.

22. Ingle, "Lighting Fires in the Belly."

23. Lynch, Grimes, and McKee, *The History of the Troubles (Accordin' to My Da)*, 55.

24. Lynch, Grimes, and McKee, *The History of the Troubles (Accordin' to My Da)*, 62.

25. Mark Phelan, "From Troubles to Post-Conflict Theatre in Northern Ireland," in *The Oxford Handbook of Modern Irish Theatre*, ed. Nicholas Grene and Chris Morash (Oxford University Press, 2016), 372–88.

Pugilists, Ponies, and Propriety

A Micro-History of Popular Athleticism at the Local Opera House

Chris Woodworth

ON NOVEMBER 18, 1896, in Geneva, New York, part of the crowd was on its feet watching the horses gallop toward the finish line. The race drew in more than twelve hundred spectators, who watched with bated breath as Cold Molasses beat the odds and drew ahead, winning the race—and its sizable purse—in a dramatic turn of events. Of course, anyone who had previously seen Neil Burgess's *The County Fair* knew that the Cold Molasses win was a foregone conclusion.[1] And while the horses were real and galloping, they were not moving around a track but instead were running on an elaborate theatrical treadmill, on the stage of Smith's Opera House. Most of the spectators were seated comfortably in their seats, with those on their feet constituting the standing-room section at the rear of the theatre. The overflowing crowd marked this event as one of the most popular and well-attended performances of the season at Smith's. But *The County Fair*'s popularity extended far beyond a one-night-only performance in a small-town opera house in rural upstate New York.

The touring nature of this now-obscure play offers a glimpse of what was popular in American theatrical entertainment at the turn of the last century. By the 1890s, local opera houses and the resultant traveling productions and touring routes were ubiquitous, which means a micro-history of one local opera house may be extrapolated to broader claims regarding regional and national trends outside of the major metropolitan destinations of the Syndicate system circuits. Individual productions and genres of performance that drew strong houses were often welcomed back for return engagements. Numerous productions brought sporting events and athletes to the Smith's stage, which indicates that athletic performances were an attractive genre for local audiences. Even so, there were limits as to how a small city or town was willing to encounter sport on its stage. *The County Fair* was one example in which audiences experienced invigorating athletic feats within the comfortable and familiar framework of melodramatic storytelling. Productions featuring equestrians and boxers performing within the often-posh settings of local opera houses, such as Smith's, elevated athletic novelty and sport to (often) profitable family-friendly entertainment. But popular athleticism also intertwined with conventions of propriety for touring acts that took to local stages at the turn of the last century. Given the salacious reputations of sites where horse races and boxing matches were customarily held, spectators were given a (usually safe) taste of transgression by attending sporting performances at their local opera house. Such performances struck a delicate balance, appealing both to the supposed conservative sensibilities of women and the presumed thrill-seeking appetites of men, revealing the boundaries of what constituted popular and suitable opera house fare featuring ponies and pugilists.

In *The Making of American Audiences: From Stage to Television, 1750–1990*, Richard Butsch charts the shifts in audience demographics and theatrical offerings in the latter decades of the nineteenth century. As women began to outnumber men, shifting from their traditional matinees to dominate the evening box office, the types of plays also shifted, with managers selecting material to appeal to their new "feminine" audiences. Simultaneously, Butsch contends this was driving men away from the theatre, which they were finding "increasingly stultifying" and therefore "began patronizing alternative pastimes." He continues, "The physical aspects of manliness, constrained by the new rules of etiquette, found an outlet in exercise and games, the gymnasium and sporting clubs. News of horseracing and boxing and adventure stories based on sports crowded out theater news in gentlemen's magazines."[2] Performances that included boxers and horses were a means of bridging some of this perceived gap in audience tastes (which were often problematically attributed to confining gender stereotypes).

Boxing matches and equestrian feats including races, exhibitions, or circus tricks were prevalent on US stages at the turn of the last century. In some communities, including Geneva, New York, the boundaries between theatre and sporting arena were blurred as "real" athletic contests, matches, games, and bouts took place on opera house stages. In *Local Glories: Opera Houses on Main Street, Where Art and Community Meet*, Ann Satterthwaite reveals that this too was a trend. She contends, "As unlikely as it might seem today, the local opera house in the late nineteenth and early twentieth centuries was once a sports arena for school, community, and professional athletes in those towns with flat-floored opera houses. . . . Wrestling and boxing, both as school sports and as professional matches, took place in the same opera houses that hosted Joseph Jefferson and the Metropolitan Opera."[3] While it may not be possible to determine what specifically led to the blurring of these boundaries between athletic arena and theatre, cultural mores, shifting audience tastes, and the agency of small-town theatre managers harmonized to bring real and fictive sport to local stages.

Early on in her foundational study of theatre audiences, Susan Bennett notes, "Cultural assumptions affect performances, and performances rewrite cultural assumptions." She later cautions against broad generalizations regarding audience appetites, asserting, "Each public will clearly have a different horizon of expectations, and these can coexist among different publics in any given society."[4] Audience demographics in New York City at the end of the nineteenth century would have been markedly different than those of small-town opera houses. Regional differences would have also likely impacted audience reception of touring companies. These variables make it impossible to discern precisely how the performances featuring sporting events and athletes within traditional melodramatic structures came to be so popular. Did that popularity emerge in larger cities and spread to rural communities or vice versa? What is clear, however, is that the recurrence of these types of performances across the US meant that theatre managers saw them as profitable ventures. This was evident in productions that toured—and sometimes returned to—Smith's Opera House in Geneva, New York.

The County Fair returned to Smith's on January 8, 1903. A few days later, the *Geneva Advertiser-Gazette* posted a short notice from the adjacent community, the residents of which often took the local rail and trolley lines to Geneva to attend events at the opera house. Although unrelated to the opera house or Burgess's production, the notice is revealing: "A protest against immoral shows and gambling devices on the Waterloo fair grounds has been filed, and probably hereafter they will be barred from the grounds. This is entirely proper in case of a county fair; it is different with a horse race."[5] Immodesty and gambling were not welcome features at an event such as a fair, where women and children were present. Yet horse races, it seems, operate under separate codes of (ir)respectability. This notice resonates with the messages of proscriptive propriety threaded throughout announcements and reviews of theatrical performances featuring boxers or equestrians. In the case of Smith's Opera House—and therefore perhaps for other local opera houses—staging sensational equestrian or boxing acts meant encountering moralistic scrutiny.

Athletic feats were deemed acceptable when removed from their customary environs of racetracks, sporting arenas, or circus big tops—illicit locations with reputations of chicanery, rowdiness, immodesty, or danger. Audiences could, therefore, safely experience a taste of these tempting and risky sites while ultimately bolstering a sense of virtuous respectability, due in part to the limits of transgression imposed by the conventions of late-nineteenth-century theatre. The confining architecture of opera houses—especially those purpose-built as proscenium theatres as opposed to music halls or other smaller venues—physically separated audience from performer, creating a clear boundary between the fictive event and the real world. The architecture of many auditoriums in larger opera houses often stratified audiences through tiered ticket pricing. Additionally, strategically marketing to women and children affirmed that the era of the raucous early-to-mid-nineteenth-century, male-dominated audiences had mostly concluded by the end of that century. Lastly, theatres often outlined clear rules of etiquette regarding audience behavior, which set opera houses even further away from the raucous crowds at horse races and boxing matches.[6] Smith's Opera House clearly advertised its "house rules" to all patrons, striving for an atmosphere of refinement and civility.[7]

The grand opening of Smith's Opera House took place in 1894 with a performance by James O'Neill in his signature role in *Count of Monte Cristo*.[8] Beginning with its opening in 1894 and continuing after its renovation to a movie palace in 1929, Smith's welcomed thousands of performance events. For the residents of Geneva and nearby smaller farming communities, Smith's provided opportunities to witness a broad array of performances including numerous productions of *Uncle Tom's Cabin*, dozens of racist minstrel shows (ranging from touring professional companies to local fire departments), political rallies, lectures, and demonstrations of early innovations in film and sound-recording technology. Notably, Smith's also welcomed touring productions by the Provincetown Players, the Washington Square Players, and the Theatre Guild.[9] These are just a few of the hundreds of examples of touring acts to grace the Smith's stage, in addition to community-created performances by local schools, colleges, and benevolent organizations. Although the records of what and who appeared are fragmented and incomplete, surviving playbills, advertising, performance reviews, ticket stubs, and newspaper articles reveal recurring themes and styles. Butsch contends, "Small towns were served by regional low-priced drama companies.... The 'blood-and-thunder' circuit, as it was called, offered heavy-handed melodrama. Every small town got its one-night stand."[10] This means that the micro-history of this one opera house serves as a snapshot of what was popular for regional and national touring circuits.

In her introduction, Satterthwaite writes, "In the fifty years after the Civil War thousands of opera houses stood proudly in small towns, with innumerable traveling performers appearing on their stages. They brought live entertainment to more towns than at any other time in US history, making this a golden age of live entertainment and also the heyday of the smalltown opera house."[11] Indeed, Brian Leahy Doyle's micro-history of the Copeland Opera House in Shullsburg, Wisconsin, reveals similar trends in type and number of performances. He attests, "While traveling troupes considered these theatres, or opera houses, the 'small time,' in these small towns the opera house nonetheless served as a symbol of civic pride and cultural aspiration as well as a public space adaptable to a wide range of theatrical and nontheatrical events."[12]

Countless local events such as dances, political rallies, and graduations were held within these spaces, making them true community centers. Residents were pleased to welcome traveling productions to their venues because they were a symbol of a small town or city's connectedness to larger artistic and cultural trends as well as a signifier of a community's value as a destination. As Ann Satterthwaite observes, "While audiences at small rural opera houses could enjoy many types of entertainment, as well as some indoor sports and community activities, their options were limited compared to the offerings in a large city. Therefore, the performers who did reach small towns attracted considerable excitement."[13] When a community had constructed a larger opera house, as opposed to the smaller halls that were popular in the early to mid-nineteenth century, there was an additional point of pride that would, as Satterthwaite contends, "reflect a town's improving economic and social status and especially its aggrandized self-image."[14] Such distinctions were made possible by theatre managers who, as Satterthwaite asserts, "became the sole arbiters of the types of performances, lectures, and plays staged at an opera house—until New York syndicates and operators shrank these managers' responsibilities to mere booking agents." This power was given to them by the entities who made construction of these venues possible, as the "entrepreneur or committee who developed the opera house usually trusted the manager to make the artistic and most of the business decisions."[15] Managers such as F. K. Hardison, who ran Smith's from its opening in 1894 until 1912, relied on resources such as *Julius Cahn's Theatrical Guides* when scheduling touring acts.

A perusal of *Julius Cahn's Theatrical Guides*, which began publication in 1896, reveals how abundant opera houses were in small cities and towns throughout the United States at the turn of the last century, as well as how touring companies booked shows with them and the means by which they traveled there. The guide offered state-by-state entries of theatres across the United States. Listings included basic theatrical specs, the name of the manager, as well as information regarding each community's hotels, newspapers, streetcars, and, most importantly, railroad access. The guide featured blank booking sheets for the season as well as ads from scenic studios, agents, theatre training academies, lighting equipment, and countless railway lines. Satterthwaite notes, "Railroads continued to be important for both transportation and promotion of the traveling show companies."[16] Companies traveling to Geneva, New York, to perform at Smith's Opera House were provided with a listing of the railway lines that serviced Geneva as well as rates for local hotels, the names of a nearby doctor and attorney, publication timelines for the local papers as well as their editors, and venue-specific information. The original Smith's Opera House contained gas and electric lighting and a proscenium stage of fair size. According to the 1897 volume of *Cahn's Theatrical Guide*, the opera house boasted a thirty-six-foot proscenium opening and a forty-foot depth, from "footlights to back wall." The guide shared the name of the opera house manager, the name of the orchestra director (W. J. Dousek), and details regarding how many copies of music to provide to the six-member orchestra. The listing also indicated what sort of print materials each company was required to prepare as well as the name of the local bill poster (N. O. Weaver) who would help advertise upcoming performances.[17] In sum, the guide offered managers and agents easy access to all pertinent logistical information to bring performances to any one of the thousands of theatres listed. As Satterthwaite asserts, "By the end of the nineteenth century, a myriad of lecturers, actors, singers, musicians, dancers, circuses, magicians, and jugglers, sometimes in a company but often alone, were traveling the rails to opera houses sprouting up in new as well as settled towns."[18] We might add athletes, specifically boxers and equestrians, to Satterthwaite's list. Much like the other genres of performance that embraced sensationalism within the confines of melodramatic plot structures, animal acts and feats of athleticism followed those patterns, therefore drawing reproof when a specific show or act veered outside of those dominant mores.

In the first three decades of Smith's Opera House, boxers took the stage in an array of events.[19] One of the most iconic boxing performances at Smith's was that of former heavyweight boxer James J. Corbett in *Gentleman Jack* in March 1895, mere months after the opera house opened. As Susan Kattwinkel contends, "When performed by real boxers, boxing on the nineteenth century popular stage can be described as a nesting doll-like series of political, physical, and metaphorical containments that allowed audiences to taste the thrill and violence of a real boxing match within the safe, framed fictionality of the expectations of the theatre."[20] The Corbett-centered melodrama was deemed unobjectionable for ladies, underscoring that even the bloodiest heavyweight champion was expected to adhere to certain parameters of respectability within the confines of theatrical convention. This melodrama was based loosely on Corbett's own biography. His nickname was "Gentleman Jim," and as Armond Fields attests, "Any similarities to Jim's real life were intentional."[21] The play featured onstage boxing in the final scene as his hero character delivered blows to the dastardly villain, a thinly veiled allusion to one of his real-life opponents in the ring. A few days later, the *Geneva Advertiser* noted that Corbett's movements were "quick as a cat's" and that the play "is not deep but it is pleasing." Papers offer conflicting accounts as to the size of the audience for Corbett's performance. The *Geneva Advertiser* asserted the performance took place in front of "an audience of fair size, but not to as full a house as had been expected."[22] The *Geneva Daily Gazette*, however, claimed, "The Corbett Company played on Friday March 29th to a packed house; curiosity to see the champion pugilist rather than any real interest in his play having served to call together people from surrounding towns as well as those in Geneva." The paper went on to contend, "The play cannot be said to possess any real merit as a creation for the stage and is evidently meant to serve only as a means of presenting the world champion of pugilism to the general public. The exhibition of bag punching by Corbett and the realistic reproduction of the prize-ring of the Olympic club, were sufficient to satisfy the mind of the truest athlete and the most ardent admirer of the fistic art."[23]

A few days after Corbett's appearance, the *Geneva Advertiser* wrote about his performance in an opera house in Oswego in which more than three hundred people were allegedly in the standing-room section because the theatre was so crowded: "He has been greeted by crowds everywhere–except in Geneva. If he could come back here, would play on a percentage, and at fifty cents a seat, the Smith Opera House would be crowded, for there is nothing about the entertainment that the most refined lady would object to."[24] Indeed, as Kattwinkel asserts, the clear boundaries between performer and audience afforded by the proscenium may have been instrumental in welcoming the "refined ladies." She writes, "The combination of fictional layering and physical orientation adjustment provided space for female and middle-class spectators to experience the thrill of proximity to professional boxers and genuine sparring within a context that was sufficiently separate from the prize ring for social and moral comfort."[25] Regardless of the actual size of the audience in Smith's Opera House in 1895 or the reason they attended, Corbett's after-performance appearance at the Alhambra, a new Geneva restaurant, brought packed crowds that spilled out onto the street (in spite of the attendees' disappointment that Corbett was shorter than they expected).[26]

Not all the names associated with boxing at Smith's were as iconic as Gentleman Jim Corbett and not all punches thrown were thrown by real-life boxers. In 1897, a touring Vaudeville duo of brothers originally from Germany—the "Rossow Midgets"—laced up their gloves. Beginning in 1892, brothers Carl and Franz Actermeier toured throughout the United States and Europe as part of the Rossow company. According to a January 1898 article in the *Pittsburgh Press*, among their celebrity boxing trainers was none other than James J. Corbett, Gentleman Jim himself.[27] The Rossow theatrical bout at Smith's was part of a larger variety performance that included comedians, musical performers, and dancers. The brothers offered exhibitions of both weight-lifting and boxing. In the lead-up to their appearance, the local papers shared the brothers' heights, noting that Franz was twenty-one inches tall while his brother Carl was twenty-nine inches tall. The *Geneva Daily Times* also noted, "The Rossows are remarkably handsome little fellows, blond, with well-cut regular features, and are perfect in all their proportions."[28] The *Geneva Advertiser* boasted, "They are real Lilliputians, athletes and midget comedians whose versatility and intelligence will compare favorably with any artist in the profession." The paper proclaimed that since they are especially attractive to ladies and children, the Opera House arranged for a special extra matinee performance to draw in that demographic.[29] Although billed as the "smallest and greatest fighters in the world," Aimee Medeiros asserts, "Due to their size, Carl and Franz were not necessarily seen as serious boxers by their audiences; rather, they were entertainers willing to risk their masculinity to please those who paid to watch them perform."[30] Unfortunately, not much more is known about the Rossows or their performance in Geneva, as the *Geneva Gazette* on January 8, 1897 wrote, "It is unnecessary to say anything further in detail concerning the midgets."[31]

Whether included as a feature in a night of variety entertainment, such as the Rossows' bouts, or framed by a conventional melodramatic script like *Gentleman Jack*, the dramatic events of performances featuring athletic prowess were presented as an athletic diversion to reassert a moral framework, rewarding the virtuous and punishing the nefarious. Satterthwaite asserts that smaller regional audiences "sought entertainment that simplified their lives and showed how traditional virtues of courage, honesty, and hard work could overcome the threats posed by societal changes." Melodrama especially supplied this, she contends, noting that "feminine virtue and traditional, often rural, values would provide the moral basis for a good life."[32] While virtue was rewarded and vice punished for the characters, the outcomes for the performers themselves were not always a foregone conclusion, however, as matters of safety and danger raised the real-life stakes. This may further illustrate the tantalizing draw for audiences. The dramatic contexts of the plays and variety performances that featured these acts were fictional, but the danger for the performers was genuine. The architecture of the theatres may have provided a safe frame for the spectators, but the real-life danger for the performers ultimately blurred the distinctions between illusion and reality. Staging feats of athletic prowess—through boxing or equestrian acts—afforded audiences heightened opportunities for exhilaration and catharsis.

Such fictively framed renditions of boxing may have contributed to shifting mores regarding real boxing matches within local opera houses. In the early twentieth century, local boxing promoter Dan Deegan faced many challenges when initially attempting to book boxing matches at Smith's. In February 1905, Deegan worked with the local Eagles club to organize a vaudeville and athletic fundraiser at the opera house to add to the coffers of their "sick and benefit fund." According to the *Buffalo Enquirer*, "a number of well-known Buffalo, New York and Canadian athletes had been engaged and tickets were readily sold at from $1 in the gallery to $2 in the boxes."[33] No punches were thrown inside Smith's, however, as "the committee was informed that the Chief of Police would not allow any boxing on the program as it was against the law." The *Democrat and Chronicle* reported that the police chief was also joined by the local sherriff in this ban. The Eagles rearranged their program, adding additional variety performances. The boxing went on, however, at a "stag entertainment" at the Eagles Hall after the performances at Smith's. Close to a thousand people witnessed a "fast, six-round exhibition of boxing" in which "the gloves weighed eight ounces and there was no ring or canvas on the floor but the boys nevertheless . . . put up an excellent contest."[34] While the demographics of the audience were not detailed in the article, presumably the designation of a "stag" event at an all-male fraternal organization implies that the majority—if not the entirety—of the audience would have been men.

The next mention of "real" boxing at Smith's appears to be in 1919. On August 13, 1919, under the auspices of the Geneva Amusement Club, Inc., Dan Deegan produced "six snappy bouts" in front of "a capacity crowd, including many women." This is a notable shift from the 1905 "stag" event, sponsored by the Eagles fraternal organization. Deegan promoted an array of sporting events over the years in Geneva, but boxing seems to have been his forte—in spite of bans intermittently outlawing it in New York State.[35] Deegan appears to have taken a break from promoting but returned boxing to Smith's Opera House in 1927; as the *Democrat and Chronicle* noted, "Dan Deegan is back in the game."[36] By 1929, the torch appears to have been passed to another local promoter, "Lefty" Louie, who produced Friday night fights in the opera house. These boxing matches would have been among some of the final performances in Smith's Opera House before it was closed for massive renovations, following its purchase by Schine Enterprises.[37] Public sentiment surrounding boxing clearly shifted between 1905 and 1927. In 1905, Deegan's bouts were exiled off-site to what would have presumably been an all-male "stag entertainment," while later matches drew men and women to the audience. Perhaps the inclusion of boxing in a variety of theatrical events specifically marketed to women and children contributed to shifting audience tastes. Indeed, in her essay on boxing and the popular nineteenth-century stage, Susan Kattwinkel concludes, "The popular stage did for boxing what theatre always does—provided space for audiences to explore it in a safe, controlled environment. The eventual result was greater acceptance of the sport and a more visceral, exciting theatrical experience."[38]

Theatre managers may have been taking a gamble with the law when inviting real-life boxing matches to the stage. Indeed, part of the lure of boxing and horse races was the opportunity to wager on outcomes. But fictive renditions of these athletic feats were clearly a safe bet for opera houses across the country, as the sheer frequency of these performances illustrates. The risks to performers, however, were anything but fictitious. Opera houses provided far more degrees of safety for patrons than the more salacious and illicit environs of most real-life boxing matches and horse races. While the audience's safety increased, however, the performers' safety remained at risk, especially performing animals. In her study of animal performances within Vaudeville,

Catherine Young notes, "Equestrian acts combined the exuberant celebration of virtuosic physical skills with clear demonstrations of control." That control came at a price, however, as "audiences enjoyed the spectacle of virtuosic animal athletes who seemed to supersede nature's intentions by balancing on tightropes and flipping in the air, largely without considering the potentially coercive training methods necessary to accomplish such feats."[39] Perhaps it was this illusion—however thinly veiled it might have been—that beguiled local audiences. Or perhaps horses onstage may have been even more enticing to theatregoers than boxing because if something went awry and a horse galloped off the stage, patrons' own safety may have been at risk and thus that potential threat further added to the exhilaration of a performance. Young also argues that the presence of animal acts onstage at the turn of the century "reminded audiences of a pre-industrial state of nature, even as the animal vaudevillians were expected to conform to modern conditions of theatrical production and were coerced to mimic human behaviours such as drunken stumbling and military marching."[40] As opera houses signaled a community's shift toward more urbane refinement, horses onstage provided a distinct reminder of rural culture's dependence upon the natural world. Whatever the reason, from theatre to circus to rodeo, equestrian drama has a long and storied history in the United States, which Kimberly Poppiti has detailed in her monograph *A History of Equestrian Drama in the United States: Hippodrama's Pure Air and Fire*. She concludes her study by noting that during "the nineteenth century, which was an age of melodrama and theatrical spectacle in the United States, the horse reached the zenith of his importance in both theatre and society."[41]

The earliest known occurrence of live horses performing at Smith's happened less than two months after the theatre's opening. On December 14 and 15, 1894, Smith's hosted the touring production of *Bartholomew's Equine Paradox*, which featured twenty-four live horses. In the run-up to the Geneva performance, the *Geneva Gazette* excerpted a review of the piece from a recent Philadelphia engagement at the Chestnut Street Opera House. The reviewer described the production and the remarkable horse performers: "The horses played school, held a trial in humorous fashion, took part in a tug of war, played the 'Last Rose of Summer,' and 'Home Sweet Home' on bells, played tag, accomplished wonderful leaps at a picnic, and every other thing imaginable, except talk."[42] Following the Geneva performances, *Equine Paradox* also graced stages in Rochester and Elmira. The hyperbolic ads for those performances boasted that *Equine Paradox* had "been praised by over one million persons! The only Entertainment patronized by all classes, and that has never had an unfavorable criticism."[43] Although the focus of *Equine Paradox* were the feats of the horses themselves, the figure(s) of their trainers could not be overlooked, particularly when they appeared onstage with them. This early occurrence of horses evidently appealed to Geneva audiences because several other productions featuring horses as a thematic focal point or as actual characters repeatedly graced the Smith's stage in the next several decades.[44] Two productions in particular featured horses and riders in moments of heightened climactic action, emblematic of the subgenre of hippodramas involving dangerous horsemanship: *Polly of the Circus* and the aforementioned *County Fair*. Much like the performances featuring boxing, these equine shows offered a glimpse of death-defying physical feats within risqué environs, all witnessed from the safety of the opera house, through the fictive lens of the plays.

Polly of the Circus began as a serial novel by Margaret Mayo and was adapted for the stage in a production of "circus and sentiment" in 1907 by Frederic Thompson, who created the production to feature his wife Mabel Taliaferro in the title role.[45] As an entry in a 1908 issue of *Theatre Magazine* noted, "Frederic Thompson looks at drama through glasses focused for Hippodrome performance."[46] *Polly of the Circus* was advertised as "A Real Circus in a Real Drama" and by 1909 the production was touring throughout the United States with its signature climactic circus scene.[47] In advance of its February 1909 appearance at Smith's, the *Geneva Advertiser-Gazette* highlighted the "most elaborate" scenic production with "circus scenes true to life, with acrobats, tumblers, clowns and trainers."[48] The titular character was a bareback rider who is injured during a performance. She recovers in the presence of a young minister, with whom she falls in love. His disapproval as well as the collective disapproval of the community leads her back to the circus, where she attempts to kill herself through a dangerous trick ride on an unfamiliar horse. She fails and instead leaves the immodesty of circus life to marry her parson beau. While many of the advance notices hail the "sensational circus ring features," the selling point for the production appears to be the sentimentality of the "play of smiles, tears and sheer joy."[49]

Polly of the Circus toured steadily throughout 1909, frequently reappearing in local opera houses, such as Smith's, which welcomed the company in both February and September. The sentimentality was noted in postings coast to coast as the production was deemed as "wholesome and teach[ing] a lesson without intending to do so" (Buffalo, New York),[50] an "effective stage sermon" with "powerful preachment on Christian charity" (Kansas City, Missouri),[51] and "a play for wives, children, sisters, sweethearts and mothers" (San Francisco, California).[52] Nowhere was the preachy sentimentality more evident than in an advance notice for the September return of *Polly* to Smith's, published in the *Phelps Citizen*, which claimed that *Polly*,

> has 138 good, hearty laughs in it—laughs which sweep through the audience like a summer breeze and cause every diaphragm between the top row in the gallery and the

front row in the orchestra to vibrate with joy. It also brings to every throat at least a dozen big gulps, and at 11 different times forces tears to the eyes of every man, woman, and child present who has eyesight and can hear. At 11 points in the play the whole audience reaches for its handkerchief, and during the succeeding moments or two the house from the stage looks like a pier crowded with friends waving farewell to an outgoing Atlantic liner. Not that the audience is waving handkerchiefs but the appearance of 1,600 people wiping their eyes simultaneously is not unlike the sight of an equal number of people wig-wagging "au revoir."[53]

Death-defying horseback feats mixed with eleventh hour redemption proved a delight to audiences across the United States. The mix of sentimentality and equestrian athleticism was already a proven formula for touring productions, as Burgess's *County Fair* had established in the early years of Smith's Opera House.

The County Fair was written by Charles Barnard and revised so many times by Neil Burgess that subsequent editions of the script listed both men as authors. Geraldine Maschio describes *The County Fair* as well as other similar melodramas as "wholesome entertainment . . . of little literary merit," noting that they were primarily vehicles for Burgess's female impersonation roles.[54] He began touring *The County Fair* throughout the United States as early as 1888. He played the central role of Aunt Abby, the "kindly spinster" who "captivated and charmed audiences and reviewers alike."[55] But Cold Molasses and the patented theatrical technology that facilitated her race win were the real stars of the show. Much has been written elsewhere about Burgess's technological innovations with treadmills and scrolling panoramas, designed to dazzle.[56] Burgess continued to develop and patent new versions of his treadmill technology. In anticipation of *The County Fair* taking the stage at Smith's Opera House in November 1896, the *Geneva Daily Gazette* wrote, "Of course the grand County Fair sweepstake continues the exciting feature of the show and when 'Cold Molasses' beats 'Ginger' and 'Rearbock,' the excitement is intense. The realism of this act is added to by the introduction of the vitascope [early motion picture projector]. It does away with the moving panorama used heretofore and gives a neat and more effective picture."[57]

The climactic horse race was a hit with Geneva audiences in 1896, with one local paper going so far as to praise the horse himself, contending that Cold Molasses "came in for his share of appreciation and he deserved it." There were other elements of the production, however, that were considerably less pleasing, starting with Josepha Crowell, who took over Burgess's signature role for a time. The *Geneva Daily Gazette* criticized her performance, proclaiming, "The immodesty of Josepha Crowell as Abigail Prue was entirely unnecessary and destroyed the effect that the true interpretation of the character would have had" and "Neil Burgess himself was more modest than the lady who takes his part." The customarily "wholesome" melodrama was anything but in the eyes of the paper: "It was very evident that the manager of the 'New County Fair' is not capable of judging the quality of an audience or he would have perceived that the introduction of indecent songs and vulgar actions are scarcely the thing to captivate a Geneva audience. If these so-called specialties constitute the 'newness' of Neil Burgess's famous play, we would emphatically advocate a return to the *Old County Fair*."[58] Luckily for Geneva area audiences, Burgess himself did appear at Smith's, when *The County Fair* returned in January 1903. His return to the role and the fact that it "comes with all the scenery and accessories that made it famous in the metropolis" and that "Mr. Burgess carries his own thoroughbred horses for the great race scene" were all part of the advance notice of the production.[59] The *Geneva Advertiser* wrote, "'The County Fair' drew the largest house of the season. There were but two vacant seats in the opera house, on the extreme front rows, but there were enough people standing behind the rails and sitting on the stairs to have filled six or eight more rows of chairs."[60] In the case of *The County Fair*, modesty was the winner and the prize was a packed theatre.

In his 1827 essay "A Plea for an American Drama," novelist James Kirke Paulding offered a critique and vision for the theatre. He argued that "dramatic exhibitions" have the power to draw audiences away from "barbarous and brutifying spectacles—from brawls, boxing-matches, and bull-baitings." For a time in the mid-nineteenth century, as women and children became a larger proportion of theatrical audiences and—as Butsch contends—men sought out physical feats elsewhere, there was a clearer distinction between real and staged fights. As the boundaries between gymnasium and theatre became more porous by the end of the nineteenth century, however, so too did the delineations between "real" and staged athleticism. In addition to his critique of "brutifying spectacles," Paulding railed against other types of spectacles in the early nineteenth century. He bemoaned how audiences seem to "require the attractions of a menagerie and a puppet-show combined, and will relish nothing living, but horses, dogs, dromedaries, and elephants prancing in the midst of pasteboard pageantry, conflagrations, bombardments, springing of mines, blowing up of castles, and such like accumulations of awful nursery horrors." Paulding laid the blame for these garish spectacles at the feet of theatre managers, therefore illustrating their inherent power to reflect and shape public tastes. With performances most evenings and afternoons, theatre managers and promoters often relied on gimmicks, celebrity, or new technology to entice audiences to local opera houses. By the late nineteenth century, the recurrence of theatrical productions and variety entertainments that showcased boxing and equestrian feats reveals that audiences had an appetite for athletic performances and their inherent danger—fictive and real.

Presumably, the popularity of such offerings by the end of the century would have left Paulding disappointed. However, he may have been pleased by the turn toward sentimentality and moralizing that marked many of the turn-of-the-century boxing and equestrian performances on opera house stages. Paulding presciently hailed the potential of the stage as "the most powerful agent in humanizing and refining mankind." He called for a national drama of comedies and tragedies featuring well-compensated, strong ensemble acting, contending that with such an approach to the stage, there "would then be no necessity to depend on perpetual novelty, which supplies the place of good acting; and perpetual shows substituted for the beautiful creations of genius."[61] As the advance notices and newspaper reviews reveal, sporting performances needed to be carefully framed within specific parameters of propriety to avoid condemnation. Audiences may glorify the athletic feats of boxers and equestrians and vicariously experience the thrill of visiting wicked sites of danger and transgression, but as Butsch notes, "critics considered theater to have a public duty not only to cultivate, but also to socialize people and, by extension, to prevent social disorder."[62] Theatre managers powerfully facilitated the frequent appearances of boxers and equestrians on the Smith's Opera House stage in Geneva, New York, as well as on hundreds of other local stages across the nation. Whether real, staged, or a hybrid of the two, countless theatrical athletic feats by pugilists and ponies toured the nation at the turn of the last century, proving their enduring popularity and moralizing reach.

Notes

1. The earliest date for *The County Fair* is 1888. It is variously referred to as *County Fair*, *The Country Fair*, and *The New County Fair*.

2. Richard Butsch, *The Making of American Audiences: From Stage to Television, 1750–1990* (Cambridge, UK: Cambridge University Press, 200): 77.

3. Ann Sattherthwaite, *Local Glories: Opera Houses on Main Street, Where Art and Community Meet* (New York: Oxford University Press, 2016), 173.

4. Susan Bennett, *Theatre Audiences: A Theory of Production and Reception*, 2nd ed. (London: Routledge, 1997), 2, 94.

5. "A Protest against Immoral Shows," *Geneva Advertiser-Gazette* (Geneva, NY), January 13, 1903, 3.

6. Richard Butsch, *The Citizen Audience: Crowds, Publics, and Individuals* (New York: Routledge, 2008), 66.

7. *Smith's Opera House* regularly published their "House Rules" in programs. These rules or notes included directives on staying seated until the conclusion

of performances and not stamping feet. For a full list of the rules, see Austin Jennings, "Smith History Blog: House Rules / House Notes," *Smith Blog*, December 10, 2018, accessed June 5, 2023.

8. Since 2018, I have been serving as the historian for our local opera house (Smith Center for the Arts, Geneva, NY [website]). I have created (in collaboration with two former students) a wide array of public-facing history events and documents, including a history blog, seasonal history tours of the building, a history-based site-specific performance event to commemorate the 125th anniversary of the building in 2019, and a YouTube series called "The Ghost Light Tours."

9. Between 1894 and the present day, Smith's Opera House changed ownership and name several times. It was purchased by Schine's Enterprises in 1927 and then renovated to a movie palace for a reopening as Schine's Geneva Theatre in 1931. Most of the aforementioned specific acts were staged at the opera house prior to the Schine's purchase. The Theatre Guild's tour of *Strange Interlude* in 1931 is one clear exception. On maps and geolocation software, the building is still designated as Smith's Opera House. For consistency's sake, I have referred to the establishment as Smith's Opera House or Smith's. For a full listing of the previous names and ownership of the opera house, consult Charles McNally, *The Revels in Hand: The First Century of The Smith Opera House, October 1894–October 1994* (Geneva, NY: Finger Lakes Regional Arts Council, 1995).

10. Butsch, *The Making of American Audiences*, 136.

11. Satterthwaite, *Local Glories*, 1.

12. Brian Leahy Doyle, "The Copeland Opera House," *Theatre History Studies* 27 (2007): 1.

13. Satterthwaite, *Local Glories* 70.

14. Satterthwaite, *Local Glories*, 210.

15. Satterthwaite, *Local Glories*, 248.

16. Satterthwaite, *Local Glories*, 73.

17. Julius Cahn, ed., *Julius Cahn Official Theatrical Guide*, vol. 2 (New York: Publication Office, Julius Cahn, 1897), 496–97.

18. Satterthwaite, *Local Glories*, 73.

19. Susan Kattwinkel, "Constraint and Violence: Boxing on the Popular Stage in the Nineteenth Century," in *Sporting Performances: Politics in Play*, ed. Shannon L. Walsh (London: Routledge, 2021), 43. In her essay, Kattwinkel enumerates the three ways in which "sparring matches and theatre came together" in the nineteenth century, underscoring that the boxing and boxing-themed events at Smith's Opera House were not merely a local phenomenon but rather indicative of national trends.

20. Kattwinkel, "Constraint and Violence," 31. Kattwinkel also goes on to analyze how the climactic fight in the play shifted meaning over time, from

"depicting a speculative version of a boxer's upcoming fight to depicting a fictionalized version of that same fight, to depicting a 'historically correct' version of a much more famous fight" as Corbett's real-life boxing intersected with performances of *Gentleman Jack* (42).

21. Armond Fields, *James J. Corbett: A Biography of the Heavyweight Boxing Champion and Popular Theater Headliner* (Jefferson, NC: McFarland, 2001), 67.

22. *Geneva Advertiser* (Geneva, NY), April 2, 1985, 3.

23. *Geneva Daily Gazette* (Geneva, NY), April 5, 1895, 3.

24. *Geneva Advertiser* (Geneva, NY), April 9, 1895, 4.

25. Kattwinkel, "Constraint and Violence," 37.

26. The Alhambra was one of many business enterprises begun by Geneva's iconic boxing promoter, Dan Deegan.

27. "The Passing Show," *Pittsburgh Press* (Pittsburgh, PA), January 23, 1898, 14.

28. "Rossow Midgets," *Geneva Daily Times* (Geneva, NY), January 9, 1897, 3.

29. "Opera House Notes," *Geneva Advertiser* (Geneva, NY), January 12, 1897, 2.

30. Aimee Medeiros, *Heightened Expectations: The Rise of the Human Growth Hormone Industry in America* (Tuscaloosa: University of Alabama Press, 2016), 56.

31. *Geneva Daily Gazette* (Geneva, NY), January 8, 1897, 2.

32. Satterthwaite, *Local Glories*, 126, 127.

33. This would have been the equivalent of roughly twenty-eight dollars and fifty-six dollars today.

34. "The Anvil Chorus," *Buffalo Enquirer* (Buffalo, NY), February 8, 1905, 8.

35. Alice Askins, "Eye of the Tiger: Dan Deegan, Part 2," *Historic Geneva* (blog), April 27, 2018, accessed June 5, 2023. Askins notes that the laws governing boxing in the late nineteenth and early twentieth centuries were in flux and that even when boxing was technically illegal, promoters like Deegan continued to produce matches, which were then covered by local newspapers.

36. "Boxing Card at Geneva Tuesday," *Democrat and Chronicle* (Rochester, NY), October 30, 1927, 17.

37. "Geneva Promoter to Stage Another Show," *Democrat and Chronicle* (Rochester, NY), October 7, 1929, 20.

38. Kattwinkel, "Constraint and Violence," 43.

39. Catherine Young, "'A Very Good Act for an Unimportant Place' Animals, Ambivalence and Abuse in Big-Time Vaudeville," in *Performing Animality: Animals in Performance Practices*, ed. Lourdes Orozco and Jennifer Parker-Starbuck (Houndmills, Basingstoke, Hampshire: Palgrave Macmillan, 2015), 87, 91.

40. Young, "'A Very Good Act,'" 78.

41. Kimberly Poppiti, *A History of Equestrian Drama in the United States: Hippodrama's Pure Air and Fire* (New York: Routledge, 2018): 179.

42. "Bartholomew's Equine Paradox," *Geneva Gazette* (Geneva, NY), December 7, 1894, 3.

43. Bartholomew's Equine Paradox in Elmira, advertisement, *Star-Gazette* (Elmira, NY), December 27, 1894, 7.

44. Horses played significant thematic roles in other plays presented at Smith's Opera House including *The Thoroughbred* (1897) and *David Harum* (1904).

45. "Polly of Circus at the Liberty," *New York Times*, December 24, 1907, 7.

46. "Liberty: Polly of the Circus," *Theatre Magazine* 8, no. 84 (1908), xi.

47. Bijou Theatre, advertisement, *The Bellman*, January 28, 1911, 122.

48. "Opera House Notes," *Geneva Advertiser-Gazette* (Geneva, NY), February 4, 1909, 2.

49. "Opera House Notes," *Geneva Advertiser-Gazette* (Geneva, NY), September 16, 1909, 2.

50. "Star," *Buffalo Enquirer* (Buffalo, NY), February 13, 1909, 7.

51. Willis Wood, "Polly of the Circus," *Kansas City Globe* (Kansas City, MO), October 18, 1909, 3.

52. "At Combination Houses," *San Francisco Examiner* (San Francisco, CA), July 25, 1909, 58.

53. "Smith Opera House: Polly of the Circus Tomorrow Night," *Phelps Citizen* (Phelps, NY), September 23, 1909, 2.

54. Geraldnine Maschio, "Neil Burgess: Female Impersonation and the Image of the Victorian Matron," *Studies in Popular Culture* 8, no. 2 (1985), 53.

55. Maschio, "Neil Burgess," 54.

56. Richard Fotheringham, *Sport in Australian Drama* (Cambridge: Cambridge University Press, 1992), 112.

57. "Amusements," *Geneva Daily Gazette* (Geneva, NY), November 13, 1896, 4.

58. "The New County Fair," *Geneva Daily Gazette* (Geneva, NY), November 20, 1896, 3.

59. "Opera House Notes," *Geneva Advertiser-Gazette* (Geneva, NY), January 6, 1903, 2.

60. *Geneva Advertiser* (Geneva, NY), November 24, 1896, 3.

61. James Kirke Paulding, "A Plea for an American Drama," *American Quarterly Review* 1 (June 1827) in *From Traveling Show to Vaudeville: Theatrical Spectacle in America, 1830–1910*, ed. Robert M. Lewis (Baltimore, MD: Johns Hopkins University Press, 2003): 159–62.

62. Butsch, *The Citizen Audience*, 68.

Contributors

Mysia Anderson (she/her) is an artist-scholar from Miami Gardens, Florida. She is an assistant professor of Black performance theory in the Department of Theatre and Dance at UC San Diego. Her forthcoming manuscript dwells on the environmental poetics of Black Miami through an exploration of oral history, storytelling, and performance. Bridging Black feminist theory and practice, she documents the city's struggle for Black sustainability in the midst of racial capitalism and environmental degradation. Mysia is also a graduate of the Atlantic Acting School's Global Virtual Conservatory. She is an actress, dramaturg, and playwright who desires to tell stories grounded in Black world-making.

Chase Bringardner, editor, is an associate provost for academic affairs and a professor of theatre at Auburn University. He is president of the Association for Theatre in Higher Education. He specializes in the study of popular entertainments such as medicine shows and musical theatre, regional identity construction, and intersections of race, gender, and class in popular performance forms. He has essays published in *Theatre Symposium*, *Studies in Musical Theatre*, and *Theatre Topics*. He most recently coedited (with Henry Bial) and contributed to *The Great North American Stage Directors, Vol. 4: George Abbott, Vinnette Carroll, Harold Prince* and contributed "Popular Provocations and Commercial Cavalcades: Popular Entertainments and the Rise of Mass Mediated Performance" to *The Cambridge Companion to American Theatre Since 1945*.

Elizabeth M. Cizmar, assistant professor of acting & directing, at Vanderbilt University, holds a PhD in drama from Tufts University and an MFA in acting from the Actors Studio Drama School. Her book project works to excavate Ernie McClintock's legacy and integrate Jazz Acting into contemporary actor training. Her published essays are featured in the *Journal of American Drama and Theatre*, *Theatre/Practice*, *The Routledge Companion to African American Theatre & Performance*, *Text & Presentation*, and *Twentieth Century and Contemporary American Literature in Context*.

Chelsea Curto is a master of fine arts in directing candidate at Baylor University. Prior to attending Baylor, Chelsea served as managing director of Wildfire Entertainment, a tech-integrated dance performance company headquartered in Singapore. Chelsea has performed internationally as an actor with Singapore Repertory Theatre, Commedia Internazionale in Florence, Italy, Granbury Theatre Company in Granbury, Texas, and many local theatres in the Houston area. Chelsea holds a BA in English from the University of Houston and began their career as a voice actor dubbing Japanese anime into English.

Janet M. Davis, keynote speaker, is a university distinguished teaching professor in American studies and history at the University of Texas at Austin. She received her BA in history from Carleton College with magna cum laude and Phi Beta Kappa honors in 1986. After working in the airline industry for several years, she received her PhD in history from the University of Wisconsin in 1998. She has taught at UT since 1998. She served as associate director of the Plan II Honors Program from 2017 to 2021. Davis is the author of *The Gospel of Kindness: Animal Welfare and the Making of Modern America* (2016) and *The Circus Age: Culture and Society under the American Big Top* (2002), and the editor of *Circus Queen and Tinker Bell: The Life of Tiny Kline* (2008). Professor Davis's current book project is a transnational cultural and environmental history of human/shark entanglements, tentatively titled *"Jawsmania": A History*. Professor Davis works regularly as a humanities consultant for museum exhibitions and documentary films, including the award-winning two-part series *The Circus*, which aired nationally on *American Experience* on PBS in 2018.

Tom Fish (he/him/his) is assistant professor of theatre history and resident dramaturg at Kennesaw State University, Georgia. His research interests include LGBTQ theatre, religion and performance, and American populist performance traditions. His articles have explored intersections of gender, sexuality, and the "miraculous" onstage, including female martyrdom in Dekker and Massinger's *The Virgin Martyr* (1622); the theatrical craft of evangelical preacher Aimee Semple McPherson; and the reception of Terrence McNally's contemporary gay Jesus play, *Corpus Christi*. Tom has previously taught at Georgia State University and Dawson College, in Montreal.

Kyla Kazuschyk, associate professor of costume technology at Louisiana

State University, holds a BA in theatre from the University of Central Florida and an MFA in costume technology from Ohio University. She has created costumes for the Orlando Magic Dance Team, the Swine Palace, the Santa Fe Opera, the Washington National Opera, the Florida Grand Opera, the Colorado Shakespeare Festival, and the Texas Shakespeare Festival. Her research on the rewarding chaos of devising was first published in the 2017 *Theatre Symposium* and was republished in the book *Creating Costumes for Devised Theatre*.

Sarah McCarroll (she/her) is a professor of theatre history and costume design at Georgia Southern University, where she also serves as the costume shop manager. A past editor of *Theatre Symposium*, Sarah's scholarship focuses on the intersection of stage costume and the historical body; her current project is a manuscript theorizing period stage costumes as vehicles of embodied memory. Sarah also serves as the chair of SETC's History/Theory/Criticism/Literature Committee. Her professional home is the Utah Shakespeare Festival, where she is a costume shop supervisor and wardrobe supervisor.

Eleanor Owicki is an assistant professor in Indiana University's Department of Theatre, Drama, and Contemporary Dance. Her research focuses on theatre in post-conflict Northern Ireland, and she is currently working on a monograph titled *Our Time, Our Place: Theatre and Civic Identity in the "New" Belfast*. Her publications include articles in *New Hibernia Review*, *Theatre Symposium*, and *Open Library of the Humanities* (#Agreement20 special issue), as well as chapters in *Theatre After Empire* and *Devised Performance in Irish Theatre*. She is the representative for the Association for Theatre in Higher Education's theatre history focus group.

Sunny Stalter-Pace, associate editor, is Hargis Professor of American Literature at Auburn University. She is writing a group biography of the performers and producers affiliated with the New York Hippodrome. Her most recent monograph is *Imitation Artist: Gertrude Hoffmann's Life in Vaudeville and Dance*.

Chelsea Taylor is a PhD candidate at Northwestern University in the interdisciplinary PhD in theatre and drama program. Her current research explores how live performances that adapt biblical stories at contemporary Christian tourist destinations across the United States function as immersive preaching techniques and conflate religious and political beliefs. Her work has been published in *Studies in Musical Theatre* and *Religion*, and as part of the *Materializing the Bible* digital scholarship project. She has been supported by the Franke Fellowship, the Mellon Interdisciplinary Cluster Fellowship, and the Buffet Travel Grant.

Chris Woodworth is a professor of theatre at Hobart and William Smith Colleges. Woodworth is coeditor of *Working in the Wings: New Perspectives on Theatre History and Labor*. Her scholarship has appeared in *Theatre Symposium*, *Theatre History Studies*, *Theatre Annual*, and a number of edited collections. Her most recent work is a public history project exploring the 127-year-old Smith Opera House in Geneva, New York, through history tours, blog posts, community-based site-specific performances, and a YouTube series. In addition to her scholarly work, she is a director and playwright. For more information on her artistry and scholarship, visit her website, This World of Yes: Theatre Writing and Artistry of Chris Woodworth.